CAREERS IN INTERNATIONAL LAW

FOURTH EDITION

Salli Anne Swartz

Cover design by ABA Publishing.

The materials contained herein represent the opinions and views of the authors and/or the editors, and should not be construed to be the views or opinions of the law firms or companies with whom such persons are in partnership with, associated with, or employed by the American Bar Association, nor of the Section of International Law, unless adopted pursuant to the bylaws of the Association.

Nothing contained in this book is to be considered as the rendering of legal advice for specific cases, and readers are responsible for obtaining such advice from their own legal counsel. This book and any forms and agreements herein are intended for educational and informational purposes only.

16 15 14 13   5 4 3

Library of Congress Cataloging-in-Publication Data
Careers in international law / edited by Salli Anne Swartz. — 4th ed.
    p. cm.
    1. Law—Vocational guidance—United States. 2. International law—Vocational guidance—United States. 3. International business enterprises—Law and legislation—United States. I. Swartz, Salli. II. American Bar Association. Section of International Law.
KF299.T73C37 2012
341.023—dc23   2012029272

ISBN: 978-1-61438-745-9

Back cover photo by Alain de Meringo, Paris, France.

http://www.ShopABA.org

Contents

Preface

Careers in International Law is now in its fourth edition and has been a perennial best seller for the American Bar Association. With legal jobs becoming more difficult to obtain and keep, I suspect that this book will remain a best seller for both law students and lawyers who are interested in finding, maintaining, or moving into a career in international law.

As you will discover, irrespective of your age, experience, nationality, residence, education, or practice area, this new edition covers more ground than the last edition. It is also inspiring, and, yes, exciting—a real page-turner for those readers who are interested in what types of career possibilities are out there in this ever-changing world of international law. Despite the challenge of securing a legal position during this economic downturn, the book provides new insight into how to use your imagination, creativity, and savvy to find that elusive job in the field of international law. It also will give you an idea of the scope of possibilities in such diverse specialties as litigation, trade, corporate, transactional, banking, financial, and maritime law, as well as positions in teaching, going in-house, and pro bono work.

The authors provide dynamic tips and strategies, as well as new perspectives and methodology, for succeeding as an international lawyer. They present many different types of careers: some are judges and professors; retired and practicing attorneys; partners with large, small, and solo firms; as well as freelance volunteers and consultants. All the authors live and practice in many different countries and work in many different languages. In this new edition, we have all shared what we believe to be helpful advice and hindsight and indispensable, yet totally diverse, advice on how to reach your goals in the vast field of international law. In addition, the authors share their analyses of how the financial crisis has changed their practice, while others have gone on to second and third careers after retiring from one profession and moving on to another one.

When I approached the task of editing this fourth edition, I thought it would be an easy one—recruiting several new authors and making certain our loyal authors would update their thoughts and insights. Yet, as with each new edition, I learned that turning ideas into print is always a challenge as well as a pleasure. It is similar to practicing international law: You need to be persuasive, not overbearing, persistent yet diplomatic, and always be creative (with a dollop of pragmatism).

As editor of this new edition, I would like to extend special thanks to our new authors for bearing with my edits and suggestions; our stalwart crew from the second and third editions for their patience and loyalty; and to Rick Paszkiet, Director of ABA Entity Book Content Publishing of the American Bar Association. Without Rick's support, suggestions, and good humor, you would not be reading this Preface today.

About the Editor

Salli A. Swartz, who is a dual national (France and United States), has practiced international business law in Paris since 1979. She began her career in Paris with the Paris-based law firm of S.G. Archibald, where she specialized for over four years in ICC arbitrations of turnkey construction projects in the Middle East. She then joined the French firm of Simeon Moquet Borde, where she acquired broad corporate law experience and was the head Anglo-Saxon attorney on several major acquisitions and joint ventures between American and French companies. She subsequently practiced with Price Waterhouse before founding Masson Piéron Swartz Beaucourt & Associés in 1988. In January 1999, she merged her practice with the firm of Phillips & Giraud, which changed its name to Phillips Giraud Naud & Swartz, and in July 2011 she created Artus Wise with a team of French attorneys specialized in litigation, arbitration, mediation, French labor and employment law; transnational business deals such as joint ventures and consortia; and French, European, and international mergers, acquisitions, and corporate and commercial law.

Her practice is quite diverse and has involved the negotiation of aircraft leases; hydrocarbon development and production agreements, mineral extraction agreements, and joint venture agreements in the hydrocarbon and extraction industries; transnational joint venture and consortium agreements; and complex industrial investments and intellectual property licensing agreements. She regularly advises French and other European subsidiaries of major American and English multinational companies in connection with their business activities in Europe, Asia (China, Japan, and India), and the Middle East and has recently advised many European and other clients with respect to compliance and other issues arising out of the Foreign Corrupt Practices Act, anti-boycott laws, and the OECD Convention on Combating Bribery of Foreign Public Officials. She is regularly lead counsel on due diligence and negotiations in connection with transnational acquisitions and mergers and has more than 20 years of experience in international arbitrations (in particular ICC arbitrations) as well as mediations (she is an accredited mediator with the Chambre de Commerce et Industrie de Paris).

She has lectured on "Structuring International Transactions: Establishing Distribution Networks" (Center for International Legal Studies, March 1996), "International Licensing and Competition Law: Know-How Licenses" (Center for International Legal Studies, October 1996), "Doing Business Worldwide: Transnational Litigation" (American Bar Association Midwest International Law Forum, November 1996), "Going International: Distribution and Agency Agreements in Europe" (Virginia Continuing Legal Education Program, May 1997), "Enforcement of Intellectual Property Rights in Madagascar" (USIA Guest Speaker, September 1997), "When Disaster Strikes—What to Do When an International Sales Transaction Goes Wrong" (International Bar Association Conference, New Delhi, November 1997), "International Mergers & Acquisitions: Critical Issues for In-House Counsel" (American Bar Association Conference, April 1998), "Rights to Privacy Worldwide: Do They Exist, Who Do They Protect and Why?" (American Bar Association Conference, April, 1998), "Transparency and Business and Government," Guest Lecturer at the Oman Chamber of Commerce and Industry and the Oman Institute of Public Administration, May 1998, "Corruption and Transparency in Business and Government," Guest Lecturer in Burkina Faso, September 1998; a Guest Lecturer in both Lomé, Togo, and Cotonou, Benin, in September 2002 and Addis Ababa, Ethiopia, in 2005 on Transparency and Corruption; gave a lecture on Legal Information Institutes in Seoul, South Korea, in August 2010; and was a delegate to the ABA International Section International Legal Exchange Program in March 2007 to Accra (Ghana), Monrovia (Liberia), and Freetown (Sierra Leone) and to Australia and New Zealand in 2009, and chaired the delegation to Jordan and Lebanon in March 2011. In March 2012, she visited Tanzania and Rwanda as part of the ILEX delegation of ABA International.

She teaches intellectual property at the Ecole National Superieur des Arts & Metiers in Paris and international arbitration and mediation at the French graduate business school Hautes Etudes Commerciales (HEC). She has also has lectured at several French law and business schools on confidentiality and ethical conflicts between French, European, and American ethical regulations.

She is the author of *Trademark Litigation in France* (Euromoney Publications, September 1996), *Litigation Strategy in France* (Euromoney Publications, March 1997), *Remedies for International Sellers of Goods* (chapter on France) (Sweet & Maxwell, 1997), and "French Language Requirements" (*International Law News*, American Bar Association, Vol. 26 no. 3, Summer 1997). She is co-editor of the book *International Joint Ventures*, published by the ABA in 2002, and an expanded second version of this book, published by the ABA in 2010. She is author of a chapter on "Selling Products in Foreign Countries–International Sales" in the book *Negotiating and Structuring International Commercial Transactions*, published by the ABA in 2003.

She is a member of the Pennsylvania and Paris bars, with specializations in the Law of International Relations and Commercial Law, and is admitted to practice before the French courts, the U.S. Court of Appeals for the Federal Circuit, the U.S. Court of International Trade, and the U.S. Supreme Court. She is the immediate past chair of the International Section of the ABA, serves on the board of directors of the Rule of Law Institute (ROLI), and is a member its Strategic Development Committee. She is also a member of the Business Law Section of the ABA, an officer of the Mediation Committee of the International Bar Association, and is the ABA liaison to the Union Internationale des Avocats. She is a member of "Femmes Business Angels" and Arbitral Women (an association of women arbitrators), co-chair of the International Fellows of the American Bar Foundation, a contributor to the Rule of Law Index 2010 of the World Justice Project, and a member of the Council on Foreign Relations.

About the Contributors

Jeffrey M. Aresty is a Massachusetts lawyer who has practiced international business and cyberlaw for 35 years (www.cyberspaceattorney.com). During that time, he first joined and then helped lead a global online network of lawyers in 35 countries, founded a new media company that distributes interactive web-based training for building and sustaining trusted online communities, and led the founding of a virtual bar association (www.internetbar.org). Jeff teaches courses on international development and online dispute resolution and cyberlaw at several universities as an adjunct professor, including the University of Massachusetts (Amherst), Bentley University, Boston University, and SMU. He has written several chapters in a textbook on cyberlaw and written chapters in textbooks on online dispute resolution and mobile technology and conflict management on furthering justice in the developing world. In his volunteer bar work, Jeff has run educational programs, published numerous articles and edited books, and led projects and committees promoting (1) the use of technology in the transformation of the practice of law, and (2) the role of cross-cultural training in international business and e-commerce.

Marcelo Bombau leads the Mergers and Acquisitions and Media and Entertainment departments of M. & M. Bomchil. Ever since joining M. & M. Bomchil in 1981, he has worked on a number of important transactions, participating actively in some of the most important reorganizations and company purchase deals carried out in Argentina during the last decade, especially related to the media and entertainment areas. Marcelo is a member of the board of directors of several local companies. He has received distinctions in several publications that distinguished him within his area of practice, has written many articles in the area of his expertise, and has lectured both in the Argentine Republic and abroad. Marcelo graduated from Universidad Nacional de La Plata in 1981. He is a member of Colegio de Abogados de la Ciudad de Buenos Aires, the American Bar Association, and the International Bar Association.

Dr. Isabella D. Bunn is affiliated with Regent's Park College, University of Oxford, and holds a professorship in ethics at the Florida Institute of Technology, College of Business. She specializes in international economic law, human rights, corporate responsibility, and global ethics. Dr. Bunn worked as a legal adviser in the public and private sectors prior to her academic career. She holds a B.S. in foreign service from Georgetown University, an M.A. in international relations, and a J.D. *cum laude* from the University of San Diego; a postgraduate diploma and M.Phil. in theology from Oxford University; and a Ph.D. in human rights law from Bristol University. She first joined the ABA Section of International Law as a student in 1978 and now serves on its Council and as Rule of Law Officer. She is also the liaison to the ABA Center for Human Rights. The advice in this chapter is based on her own experiences and those of her students over the years. She is delighted for this opportunity to encourage the next generation of international lawyers, and she looks forward to meeting readers at an upcoming event of the ABA Section of International Law.

Michael E. Burke was the Chair of the 25,000-member American Bar Association Section of International Law for the 2011–12 year and is a partner of Arnall Golden Gregory, LLP in the Washington, D.C., office on the Corporate Practice team. He is an editor and co-author of the *Corporate Counsel's Guide to Doing Business in China*, 3d ed., and is the United States Country Councillor for LAWASIA.* He also serves on the board of directors of the India China America Institute. Michael focuses his practice on cross-border transactions, including joint ventures, strategic alliances, private equity investments, mergers and acquisitions, distribution and reseller networks, and technology licensing. He also advises clients on compliance with U.S. export controls regulations, U.S. economic sanctions programs, the Foreign Corrupt Practices Act, and U.S. antiboycott regulations. Michael counsels clients on U.S. and international privacy, data protection, and information security issues, and represents clients before the Federal Trade Commission in connection with information security investigations.

---

* LAWASIA is an international organization of lawyers' associations, individual lawyers, judges, legal academics, and others that focuses on the interests and concerns of the legal profession in the Asia Pacific region.

Michael Marks Cohen has been in private maritime law practice in New York City since 1970, specializing in admiralty law and international arbitration, and is currently of counsel to Nicoletti Hornig & Sweeney. He taught the admiralty course at Columbia Law School for more than 30 years. A Titulary Member of the Comite Maritime International, he is an elected member of the American Law Institute, which honored him with the John Minor Wisdom Award. Michael is a former member of the Executive Committee of the Maritime Law Association of the United States, a former Development Officer of the ABA International Law Section, and a former member of the Documentary Committee of the Baltic & International Maritime Council (Copenhagen).

Diane Penneys Edelman is Director of International Programs and a Professor of Legal Writing at Villanova University School of Law, where she has taught since 1993. She served as Co-Director and then Assistant Dean for Legal Writing from 2000 through 2008. She directs the summer program in Rome co-sponsored by Villanova Law and University of St. Thomas School of Law, and has taught International Art & Cultural Heritage Law in that program. In addition, she advises students regarding study abroad, and assisted in the development of and supervises Villanova's JD/LLM International Studies programs. Diane regularly teaches International Advocacy, a unique legal writing course for first-year law students. She has written and spoken regionally and nationally about legal writing, the connection between international law and legal writing, and teaching legal writing to students whose first language is not English. She has served as a Fulbright Specialist at European Humanities University in Vilnius, Lithuania, and is currently a Co-Chair of the ABA Section on International Law's International Legal Education and Specialist Certification Committee. She has also served on the Editorial Board of *Legal Writing: The Journal of the Legal Writing Institute* and the Board of the Association of Legal Writing Directors, and has chaired the International Legal Exchange Section of the Association of American Law Schools. She is currently President of the Lawyers' Committee on Cultural Heritage Preservation. Diane earned an A.B. in Near Eastern Studies from Princeton University and a J.D. from Brooklyn Law School, where she was Editor-in-Chief of the *Brooklyn Journal of International Law*. She also clerked for the Honorable I. Leo Glasser of the U.S. District Court for the Eastern District of New York, and was a litigation attorney at Stroock & Stroock & Lavan in

New York and at Hoyle, Morris & Kerr in Philadelphia before teaching at Villanova Law. She also serves as faculty advisor for the Law School's Art Law Society, the Philadelphia Volunteer Lawyers for the Arts, and Barnes Foundation externships.

Jeffrey B. Golden is Chairman of The P.R.I.M.E. Finance Foundation in The Hague and a member of the Foundation's Panel of Recognised International Market Experts in Finance, a Visiting Professor in the Law Department at the London School of Economics and Political Science, and a Director of MFX Solutions, Inc., an industry initiative providing currency hedging for microfinance. He recently retired from international law firm Allen & Overy LLP, which he joined as a partner in 1994 after 15 years with the leading Wall Street practice of Cravath, Swaine & Moore. He was the founding partner of Allen & Overy's U.S. law practice and senior partner in the firm's global derivatives practice and has extensive experience in a wide range of capital markets matters. He acts for the International Swaps and Derivatives Association, was a principal author of ISDA's master agreements, and has appeared as an expert witness in several high-profile derivatives cases. Jeffrey is Chair of the Society of English and American Lawyers (SEAL), a former Chair of the American Bar Association's Section of International Law, and a Life Fellow (Co-chair, International) of the American Bar Foundation. He also serves on the Steering Committee of the ABA/UNDP International Legal Resource Center, on the ABA Commission on Ethics 20/20, and as a member of the ABA House of Delegates.

Carolyn Herzog is the Vice President and Head of legal for Symantec Corporation's Europe, Middle East, and Africa region. In this capacity, Carolyn manages legal strategies and support for Symantec's business in the region including all areas of compliance. Symantec, a Fortune 500 company with over $6 billion in revenue, is a global leader in providing security, storage, and systems management to customers that include consumers, small businesses, and the largest global organizations. Symantec operates in more than 50 countries with over 20,000 employees worldwide and maintainins strong governance and ethics policies and procedures. Prior to her current role, Carolyn managed the legal support for other areas of Symantec's business, including the Global Services and Support organization, IP, Marketing and trade compliance, based out of the Washington, D.C. area. Before joining Symantec in December, 2000, Carolyn was the general counsel for

AXENT Technologies, and worked in the international development arena, both in the nonprofit sector and with the World Bank in Washington, D.C. She currently lives in London with her husband and two children.

Bruce Horowitz was born and raised in the town of Galion, Ohio, and has degrees from Brandeis University (B.A. history), NYU Law (J.D.), and Universidad Catolica, Quito (diploma superior in anti-corruption). After living in Ecuador for 30 years, Horowitz considers both Ecuador and the United States as home. He is a founder and managing partner of the Paz Horowitz Robalino Garcés law firm in Quito. Bruce is a long-time member of the American Bar Association and has been active in the ABA Section of International Law and its committees on International IP (former chair), Latin American & Caribbean (former vice-chair), Lawyers Abroad (former chair), and Anti-Corruption (former co-chair). He is also active in the International Trademark Association (INTA). Bruce has been recognized internationally for his leadership in intellectual property and for his anti-corruption/anti-extortion work.

Judge Marilyn J. Kaman, a state court trial judge for the Fourth Judicial District in Hennepin County, Minnesota, since 1990, was selected in 2002 by the United Nations to become an international judge for the UN Mission in Kosovo, where she adjudicated cases following cessation of the 1999 hostilities in the war-torn region. In June 2011 she was elected by the UN General Assembly to serve as an ad litem judge from the United States to serve on the newly created UN Dispute Tribunal. From 2011 to 2012 Judge Kaman adjudicated employment disputes within the United Nations pursuant to this appointment. Judge Kaman has extensive experience as a trial court judge, with emphasis on major criminal trials and major civil litigation. Additionally, she has had specialty court assignments for probate, mental health, and family court divisions of the court. Judge Kaman is a member of the American Bar Association and has held the following appointments: ABA alternate representative to the U.S. Mission; ABA Representative to ECOSOC; ABA Section of International Law—Membership Officer, Publications Officer, co-chair, UN & International Institutions Coordinating Committee; editor-in-chief, *International Law News*; co-chair, International Criminal Law Committee; among other appointments.

Andrew J. (Josh) Markus is a shareholder at Carlton Fields, P.A., in its Miami office. He is the chair of the International Practice Group of the firm. He is also a past chair of the ABA's Section of International Law and a Delegate-at-Large to the House of Delegates of the ABA. His practice involves representing U.S. and non-U.S. companies in the United States and worldwide in international and domestic corporate transactions, including joint ventures, strategic alliances, mergers and acquisitions, and financial transactions. Josh frequently coordinates multijurisdictional projects for major U.S. and non-U.S. companies.

Janet H. Moore practiced international business law for 15 years at a multinational law firm, a Fortune 100 company, and as a foreign visiting attorney, a premier Mexico City firm, before launching her Global Rainmaking® consultancy (www.GlobalRainmaking.com). As a professionally trained and certified executive coach (www.InternationalLawyerCoach.com), she helps lawyers succeed with customized client development, branding, and career strategies. Janet also teaches professional services marketing and related topics at Rice University's Jones Graduate School of Business.

Homer E. Moyer, Jr. is a partner at Miller & Chevalier, where he founded the firm's International Department and manages a diverse international regulatory and litigation practice. A former chair of the Section of International Law, Homer was the co-founder and chair of CEELI, the ABA's Central European and Eurasian Law Initiative, and the founder of the CEELI Institute in Prague. A political appointee in both Democratic and Republican administrations, Homer served as General Counsel, Counselor to the Secretary, and Deputy General Counsel of the U.S. Department of Commerce. Before government, he practiced with Covington & Burling; wrote *Justice and the Military,* a treatise on military law; and served in Navy JAG, with collateral duty at the White House. He has received the ABA's World Order Under Law Award and was honored at Runnymede during the rededication of the ABA Memorial to Magna Carta. A member of the Council on Foreign Relations, past president of the Washington Council of Lawyers, and father of four, he also authored the best-selling book *The R.A.T. (Real-World Aptitude Test): Preparing Yourself for Leaving Home* (Capital Books, 2001).

Priscilla B. Pelgen is the founder and principal attorney of her Indiana firm, The Law Office of Priscilla Pelgen. She also owns and operates http://www.ilawyerindiana.com, a virtual law firm, and http://www.mysuccessfromscratch.com, a mentoring and coaching business teaching lawyers how to build their own practices from scratch. Ms. Pelgen is one of America's PremierExperts™ for eLawyering in business and marketing in the new economy. She is also a popular speaker and author on the topics of eLawyering, business building in the new economy, and men's custody, divorce, child support, and parenting time issues. Priscilla has been seen on CNN, FOX NEWS, MSNBC, CNBC, as well as NBC, CBS, ABC, and FOX affiliates and featured in *The Wall Street Journal.* She is the author of five books, including *The Ultimate Pre-Divorce Playbook for Men* (available on Amazon). Priscilla received her bachelor's degree from Indiana University and her law degree from Oklahoma City University School of Law. She is admitted to bars of the state of Indiana, and the United States District Court, Northern and Southern Districts of Indiana. She is active in the Kokomo, Indiana, community, both professionally and personally. In addition to participating on bar association committees, she is a member of the Board of Trustees for the Howard County Historical Society. Priscilla balances her time between practicing law, writing, coaching, bodybuilding, riding her motorcycle, and spending time with her family. She is married to David, and mother of Cody, Ciera, Brooklyn, and Reece. She has five chihuahuas, Lola, Chewy, Dori, Cleo, and Tink.

Mary Noel Pepys has significant years of legal experience in the private and public sectors. She has lived and worked abroad for the past 19 years, since 1993, within the former Soviet Union, Eastern Europe, the Middle East, and Asia providing legal and technical assistance to national governments, judiciary, bar and law faculties. With her knowledge of common law and civil law principles, she has successfully developed, managed and implemented effective legal reform projects, promoting transparent and fair justice systems in more than 40 countries. She has worked with the American Bar Association, the U.S. Agency for International Development, the U.S. Department of State, The World Bank, and the United Nations Development Programme. From 2008 to 2009, Pepys served as the Justice Advisor at the Bureau of International Narcotics and Law Enforcement Affairs in Afghanistan for the U.S. Department of State. Previously, Pepys worked in San Francisco at Heller, Ehrman, White & McAuliffe and at her own law firm as a land use attorney; served as a legal officer for the international peacekeeping force, Multinational Force and Observers, headquartered in Rome, which oversees the security arrangements of the 1978 Camp David Peace Accords; and worked in Washington, D.C., as the Special Assistant to Ambassador Daniel J. Terra at the Department of State, and for Congressman Henry S. Reuss, Chairman of the Committee on Banking, Finance, and Urban Affairs. Due to her private and public sector experience, Governor Edmund G. Brown recently appointed Pepys to the UC Hastings College of the Law Board of Directors.

Aaron Schildhaus is an international corporate and business lawyer specializing in commercial transactions, trade, and finance. He was chair of the ABA's Section of International Law in 2008-2009. Aaron has written and lectured on international relations, policy, and trade throughout the United States, Europe, Africa, the Middle East, and Asia, and is an expert on anti-corruption matters, human rights, and the rule of law. He has extensive corporate and legal experience representing major multinational corporations, as well as small and medium-sized investors, based in Europe, the United States, and elsewhere, with respect to transnational corporate strategy, international sales and distribution, transborder business alliances and joint ventures, and international transactions and trade in the United States and abroad. Aaron was a member of the corporate law department of PepsiCo, Inc. for three years before moving to Paris in 1975, where he practiced for the next 10 years. He was founder and president of The International Business Law Firm and The European Business Law Firm, and was of counsel to the firm of Carlsmith Ball in its Washington, D.C., office. Since 1996, he has been in private practice, with offices in Washington, D.C., and Buenos Aires.

Mark E. Wojcik is a professor of law at The John Marshall Law School in Chicago, where he has taught public international law, international business transactions, international trade law, international human rights, international organizations, and lawyering skills. He also teaches law in Switzerland (at the University of Lucerne Faculty of Law) and in Mexico (at the Facultad Libre de Derecho de Monterrey). He served as publications officer for the ABA Section of International Law, editor of the section's newsletter, and editor of the section's international law year-in-review, *The International Law News*. He chaired the Association of American Law Schools Section on International Law, Section on North American Cooperation, Section on International Human Rights Law, Section on Graduate Programs for Foreign Lawyers, and Section on International Legal Exchange. Mark previously chaired the Illinois State Bar Association (ISBA) Section on International and Immigration Law and served the ISBA Board of Governors. He is also chaired the American Society of International Law Interest Group in Teaching International Law and the Teaching International Law Committee of the American Branch of the International Law Association. He is the founder of the Global Legal Skills Conference Series. He previously clerked at the Supreme Court of Nebraska, the U.S. Court of International Trade, and the Supreme Court of the Republic of Palau.

Janet B. Wright is Vice President, Corporate, Securities & Finance Counsel and Assistant Secretary at Dell Inc. She is primarily responsible for Dell's corporate securities, corporate finance, corporate governance and general corporate matters, and also has responsibility for legal department operations. In prior roles at Dell she had responsibility for Dell's small and medium business sales segments as well as the Americas channel sales business, for the consumer and small business segments and the related global customer contact centers, and for privacy and data protection matters. Prior to joining Dell, Ms. Wright was in private practice. During that period, she focused on mergers and acquisitions, equity structuring and choice of entity issues, and international and domestic tax work. She is a member of the ABA Section of International Law and Practice and the Tax Section. She is the former chair of the International Section's Women's Interest Network.

Profile of the ABA
Section of International Law

Who Are We?

- We are over **23,000 members** in over **90 countries**.
- **More than 50% of our members are in private practice:** The top three areas of practice: business law, litigation, and intellectual property.
  - Corporate Counsel—more than 12% are U.S. members
  - Government Lawyers—3% are U.S. members
  - Academics—4% are U.S. members
- **You don't have to be a U.S. lawyer to be a member of the Section!**
  - 18% of members are non-U.S. qualified lawyers
  - 18% of members are U.S. qualified lawyers practicing abroad

Where Are We?

- **U.S. lawyers in the U.S. (top 5):** Washington, D.C., New York, California, Texas, and Illinois
- **U.S. lawyers abroad (top 5):** United Kingdom, Japan, China, Canada, and Germany
- **Non-U.S. lawyer abroad (top 5):** Canada, United Kingdom, Brazil, Germany, and Australia

What Do We Do?

We serve our members, the profession and the public through:

- **Continuing Legal Education:** Seasonal meetings; stand-alone; committee programs; teleconferences, webinars (e.g., the Section's four-day in-person annual Spring and Fall Meetings, the annual "Live from the SEC" videoconference; in-person Committee programming such as the "International Families: Money, Children and Long-Term Planning" in Washington, DC, stand-alone meetings partnering with foreign bar associations such "Law, Business and Society – US/Israel/Global Relationships" in Eilat, Israel, teleconferences such as "Anatomy of an M&A Deal,")

- **Member Publications:** *The International Lawyer*, themost widely circulated law review/law journal on internationallaw in the world; the *International Law News,* a quarterly magazine; and 25 committee newsletters relating to International Human Rights, Latin American/Caribbean, China, Asia/Pacific, and International Family Law
- **Book Publications** on international practice issues
- Over **60 substantive committees in 12 divisions**, with active listserves facilitating current information exchange among experts in the specific areas covered by the committees
- **ABA United Nations Development Program International Legal Resource Center**
- **International Outreach to the Global Legal Community:**
  - We organize ABA Day at the United Nations
  - We have liaisons to the World Trade Organization, as well as to Foreign and International Bars
  - We send delegations on International Legal Exchange (ILEX) trips, and have visited 50 countries since 1982
  - Annual International Bar Leaders Trips: Our Section Leaders travel to different countries to meet with and develop relationships and cooperate with foreign bars.
- **Interaction with the U.S. Government:**
  - Annual dinner of General Counsels of U.S. Government Departments and Agencies
  - State Department Lawyers on Section Council
  - Advice on nominations to international courts
- **Policy Developer and Advocate**
  - Numerous reports and recommendations that create official ABA policy (e.g., endorsing the UN *Protect, Respect and Remedy* human rights framework, encouraging courts to respect data protection laws of sovereign countries, opposing laws that prohibit the use of foreign law by domestic courts)
  - Blanket Authority Comments

Part 1

Foreign Practice

How Do You Get from Philadelphia to Paris?

by Salli A. Swartz

A. Introduction

Other than the fact that both cities start with the same letter and I was born in one and live in the other, the practice
of law in Philadelphia and Paris is as different as a Philly
steak sandwich and a steak frites. They both have meat
and a baguette-like bread, but they do not taste anything
alike. After living and working in Paris for the last 33 years,
I still ask myself how I got here and how I did what I did.

For those readers who have not read the third edition
of this book, I will summarize my unpredictable and un-
foreseeable career path and then reflect on the bigger picture, which hopefully will give you some insight into your
current and future career paths.

The job market when I started looking for legal work
in 1977 and the legal job market today are so different
that I will point out some obvious and a few not so obvious differences and give some (hopefully not too outdated)
tips on how to succeed in 2012.

B. The Beginnings

I was always fascinated with Europe and international law
and had spent my junior year abroad in Paris. I fully in-

3

tended to find a way to live and work abroad; I just didn't know if it was law that would provide the ticket to get there. Although I was seriously interested in international law as a career option, I dropped it in about 10 minutes when I considered my options upon graduation from law school in 1977.

At that time and at my law school, there were only a few courses in international law, and they concentrated on public international law. The law school did offer a certificate in International Legal Studies for those who took all of the courses, which I obtained. I was also the lead articles editor of the *Journal of International Law and Commerce.* The availability of international law courses in ABA-accredited law schools today is clearly much different from what I experienced, and, as you will see from reading the other chapters in this book, opportunities abound to study international law in all of its facets both in the United States and, even more interesting, in summer and exchange programs abroad.

The only job recruiters who came to the school were the New York corporate firms, which were not interested in anyone who wanted to practice international law, unless it was after seven years of learning the ropes in mergers and acquisitions (M&A), corporate taxation, and litigation. Public international law jobs were almost nonexistent. The United Nations entities had (and still have) national quotas, which were filled with American nationals; and NGOs were few and far between and did not have funding to pay anyone with outstanding student loans. Working for the U.S. government at the height of the Vietnam era was not on my agenda.

So I put the idea of a career in international law aside, thinking that I would make it a hobby by reading and doing pro bono work. Instead, I became a legal services attorney in rural Pennsylvania. This option suited me quite well, but with the drastic decreases in Legal Service Corporation funding, opportunities in this sector are dwindling. The 1970s were boon years for poverty law, and I thrived in that activity. But it is funny how things turn out. The ticket to Europe wasn't law, it was love: I married a French engineer and agreed to go with him to Paris while he was being trained by the French parent company of his U.S. employer.

End of fantasy, beginning of struggle.

C. The Struggle

How do you obtain employment in a country where your language skills can just about get you through the market and the appetizer at a dinner party, but not through a serious job interview, never mind any legal research or writing? How do you obtain a job with a corporate law firm when your only background is U.S. poverty law? How do you get admitted to practice when there are two professions, *conseil juridique* and *avocat,* and the former required gainful employment with an existing firm of *conseil juridique* and at least three years' prior practice and the latter required French nationality and a French bar exam? How do you do all of this with no mentors and no contacts? The only answer I came up with at the time was to send out 200 resumés, call everyone in the phone book, and be persistent. I even knocked on doors. (Note: This is not a good idea.) This was before the Internet and even before computers. The choices were slim. Today the choices are myriad, provided that you bring something to the proverbial table of the firm, NGO, government, or company. That something can be language proficiency(ies), contacts (yes, this still helps), cutting-edge specialization in emerging areas of the law, or any other experience that can differentiate you from other candidates and help the organization with which you want to work. Also consider doing something broadening—such as joining the Peace Corps, for example—before you try to become a human rights lawyer. Explore opportunities to travel and develop contacts in an area of the world where law firms want to sell their skills. It is up to you to come up with a resumé that is going to make the difference for you.

D. The Breakthrough

After two weeks, I had my first offer: babysitting the telephones, faxes, and telex for a firm of two lawyers, both of whom were going on vacation—it was August in Paris—and I took it. After one month, I had an offer to do expatriate tax returns with Peat Marwick. I took it. After eight weeks, I resigned from the tax position and accepted an offer as an international arbitration paralegal with an Anglo-Saxon law firm in Paris. Not great for an attorney with three years of experience, but my foot was in the door, and at the time, anything looked better to me than sitting on the 22nd floor of a skyscraper in the La Defense part of Paris filling out tax forms for expatriates.

After three months at the law firm and several persuasive arguments, I was promoted from paralegal to attorney. After six months, I was interviewing witnesses in Finland and drafting claims for International Chamber of Commerce (ICC) construction arbitration in the Middle East. After two years, I was formally admitted to practice as a foreign *conseil juridique* and had the official working papers to go with the title. After four years, I was knee-deep in technical construction claims in several ICC construction arbitrations in the Middle East and realized that I needed to learn French corporate and commercial law. I decided to resign and look for a position with a French firm of *avocats*.

In those four long years, I had progressed from a paralegal position to an experienced ICC arbitration attorney and now had sufficient confidence, language skills, and cultural and legal knowledge to obtain a position with a French firm of *avocats*. I no longer felt like an American duck out of water. I had become Parisian. Eureka! I screamed with joy. I had finally made it—or so I thought.

What made my job search back then different from what many of you are going through today? The quick response is, not much: Candidates like me were a dime a dozen in Paris (i.e., American expatriates looking for a legal job), and I had nothing to distinguish me from many others who had Harvard or Yale on their resumés. Or better, already had employment with New York firms that had Parisian offices.

How did I make it work in a market that was not unlike the one that exists today—too many candidates for far too few jobs? I think it was my willingness to take almost anything that came my way. Clearly, the financial crisis has now taken a toll on the availability of jobs in the legal market. The legal market has changed, in my opinion, irreversibly. Read on to see how to digest this fact and make it work for you.

E. Success Is Just Around the Corner

Changing firms, not unlike changing spouses (not that I have any experience), is always interesting, particularly when you do it on the rebound. The firm I joined was a small boutique firm with three partners. I was the second American; the first one was writing a Matthew Bender publication, *Doing Business in France,* for the firm. When the book was finished, he left.

I understood that I was hired to be an associate who would work on client files with other attorneys and the clients they represented; they understood that I would be the linguistic specialist and would spend my days correcting English-language documents drafted by the French (male) attorneys, who did not take kindly to corrections. So much for clear communications.

The firm was chauvinistic and somewhat anti-American: This was France in the 1980s. I was told by one partner one evening when I was working late to go home and cook dinner for my husband; another partner informed me that he could not put me on the arbitration team because the client did not want to work with a woman. Ah, the joys of working in a foreign environment. Despite the setbacks and frustrations, in the next four years I spent with that firm, I learned French corporate, labor, and commercial law, and my written and spoken French became fluent, albeit accented. It was an essential step, even if it wasn't exactly the perfect fit.

I left that firm to join an offshoot of Price Waterhouse, where I was a senior attorney. The experience was interesting and challenging, but there I was with an accounting firm again. Not my cup of tea. What was my next step?

What is anyone's next step? For me it was finding a job that made sense to me and gave me back at least as much as I would give. I was looking for certain criteria in a job, which can be measured somewhat objectively: independence, intellectual challenges, and the chance to build something for my clients and myself with very little distance between us.

But today's market is vastly different from the one I encountered. An entire category of legal work that I was trained to do, wanted to do, and have been doing for over 30 years has been "downgraded" to non-lawyers, and it is likely it will never again be a profit center in law firms. The work has disappeared through outsourcing (often abroad), the use of skilled in-house paralegal professionals (contract managers, for example, who do not have law degrees), and more senior associates supervising paralegals in law firms. Thanks to the financial crisis, millions of lawyers who previously had been gainfully employed are either out of work or are underemployed internationally. Their jobs don't exist anymore because of technical revolutions, or they are being done by a workforce that is less skilled—e.g., the disappearing secretary replaced by a computer and good software; the paralegal replacing an attorney; the local IT person replaced by a hotline in a developing country; the librarian replaced by online research tools; the "baby" associate doing book research replaced by the paralegal doing research on the Internet. It's all about the bottom line here, not necessarily the best service.

The categories of services that are performed less and less by skilled experienced lawyers and more and more by skilled in-house paralegals are (i) contract drafting and negotiations for companies that have their pre-established list of dos and don'ts; (ii) due diligence done by outside law firms for companies in connection with ethics, corruption, and other compliance issues (which is now done by compliance officers in most cases, at least for the first round of investigations); and (iii) due diligence/audits for mergers and acquisitions (often done through off-shore outsourcing by non-lawyers; litigation management (again, often through off-shore outsourcing); and other types of advice-driven counsel. Litigation and pre-litigation audits and investigations remain high on the list of "cannot do without" lawyers once a prosecutor gets involved, but not researching and writing long, detailed memoranda to evaluate business and legal risks.

When you engage in a legal job search today, try to remember that law firms are not the same places they were over the past 30 years. No matter how they market themselves to candidates, clients, or more generally to the outside world, big law firms pray to one core value: profits per partner. They don't need junior associates doing the work junior associates used to do because they can outsource it to less expensive non-lawyers. Yes, there are supervision, quality, and potential liability issues, but the jobs are lost, and it does not look like they are coming back. Moreover, the Internet has completely changed access to the law and to lawyers, and to the documents they used to handcraft for each client. Forms abound free of charge. Clients will not pay for rehashed advice they think they can find without you.

So you need to create your profile in light of what firms and businesses are looking for now, not what you thought they were looking for even five years ago. And we all need to remember that we are a service industry: If we don't have what someone needs, we will become obsolete.

F.   The Jump to Independence

When a friend and colleague was admitted as an *avocat,* she suggested that we start a firm. I burst out laughing at the mere suggestion that I could earn a living on my own. Six months later we were profitable, and although the firm has grown and moved and my original partner is long gone, it is still independent and successful more than 25 years later.

One of the reasons I believe my firm has been so successful and has lasted so long is that my focus and expectations were always very clear. Having experienced several different types of legal practices, I knew what I wanted: independence and an exciting and varied practice. I was much less interested in firm politics, money, security, and power than with the challenge of every day being a new learning experience. Flexibility, adaptability, and loyalty to my clients were and are the keys to my success. I have always focused on what I think is the most important part of a law practice: making the client happy by being efficient, amiable, and business-like. Solve the client's problem efficiently, intelligently, and with good humor, and you cannot go wrong.

My first partner and I did not spend a lot of time or effort trying to put together a marketing plan; we did not have the time and were sorely lacking in expertise. But we did do what came naturally, which was network, network, and network. This was pre-Internet and pre-email and pre-the "electronic age." We traveled and attended conferences and cocktail receptions and spread the word amongst our family, friends, and client contacts. Not the best marketing plan in the world, but it worked for us in 1988. Our motto at the time was "Be available, accessible and cost-effective." We innovated billing practices to differentiate ourselves: in 1988 no one was offering fixed flat fees, average fees, monthly budgets, and the like. We did (and my firm still does).

I became active in the International Section of the American Bar Association and began making friends and writing articles in the *International Law News.* I also wrote chapters in books on my interests (joint ventures, mergers and acquisitions) and participated in seasonal meetings as a panelist or moderator on programs that promoted my expertise. My partner chose another association, so we spread the networking around to different groups. Happy clients will refer others to you. You can and should leverage that goodwill by providing your clients with free updates on legal issues that could affect their businesses via seminars and newsletters; reasonable negotiated billing practices; and any other ideas you may have to stay in touch.

In line with my objectives, my practice has varied over the years with the one underlying constant: diversity. I have not specialized and do not intend to do so. I go where my clients want to go, and I specialize in their activities.

The matters I have handled have varied over the years and include the following:

- Purchasing and leasing of aircraft for a new Middle East airline
- Finding and negotiating the purchase of chateaux and other high-end real estate for foreign individuals, including a vineyard in Burgundy
- Consortia agreements for the construction of military air-bases
- Hydrocarbon exploration and exploitation agreements for oil and natural gas fields in Africa and the Middle East
- Complex international software framework license agreements
- Capital risk investments and licensing arrangements for high-tech start-ups
- Construction contracts for high-speed motorboats for a government and a luxury sailboat for an individual
- Distribution, joint venture, and agency agreements for construction of stadiums and train systems
- Conducting international arbitrations as counsel and as arbitrator
- Acting as a mediator
- Litigating labor lawsuits and intellectual property infringement cases
- Negotiating with French unions in lockout and strike situations
- Mergers and acquisitions of French companies by Anglo-Saxon companies
- Acquisitions by French companies of Swiss, African, German, Austrian, Italian, English, American, Israeli, Indian, and other foreign companies
- Teaching international arbitration and mediation and intellectual property in French business and engineering schools

I have met interesting people in interesting places. I have traveled to the Middle East covered from head to toe in black. I have eaten alone in restaurants and was mistaken for a lady of the evening in the coffee shop at the Hilton in Rotterdam, The Netherlands, in 1981. I have been subjected to jokes about women, Jews, racial minorities, and other off-color and not-very-funny remarks. I have tried to get a sense of conversations in languages I did not understand by watching the eyebrows, hands, and body language of the speakers. I hitchhiked a ride to the airport when my clients forgot me at the hotel and the taxis were on strike. I have been sequestered by unions that occupied a factory. I have eaten unrecognizable food and slept in less-than-ideal hotels.

But I have never (well, almost never) been bored and delight in the fact that I am constantly learning about new laws, new issues, new languages, and new cultures. It's a challenge and can be exhausting, but most days I would not trade it for any other profession in any other country.

And just when I thought I was finished with changes and after I finished my term as Chair of the Section of International Law of the American Bar Association in August of 2011, I decided to join a team of younger French attorneys to start a new law firm. Most people (at least in France) are focusing on retirement and certainly would not take on such a challenge at the ripe age of 59, but there I was, asking for more stimulation and challenges.

What fun and joy to be with enthusiastic lawyers who want to build a firm. What an intellectual and emotional challenge to find common ground with a new team and discuss cross-marketing our respective skill sets. I encourage everyone to consider taking the leap into the unknown, even if you are settled into a routine and feel safe and satisfied. Nothing can stimulate more than the challenge of creation.

G. How to Prepare for a Career in International Law

As you prepare for a career in international law, you will need to consider what type of international law you want to practice, in what environment, and what type of lifestyle you want to live.

1. What Is International Law?

You can't prepare for something if you don't know what it is. I will share a secret with you: A career in international law means something different to every one of us who are in the field. It could mean working in a law firm in a foreign country, or working in a law firm in the United States and dealing with foreign clients, or negotiating deals between clients located in two different countries as either in-house counsel for a multinational company or as an attorney with a law firm with clients based in different countries in the world.

It can also mean working for a U.S. government agency dealing in international public law matters, such as the State Department, or international private law matters, such as the Commerce Department, or it could mean working in the military as a Judge Advocate General (JAG) officer, or for a nongovernmental organization (NGO) abroad, or as a staff attorney with a United Nations organization, such as ILO, WHO, WIPO, or UNESCO. It can also mean being part of the defense or prosecutorial team(s) of the International Criminal Court, another type of hybrid international court dealing with war crimes, or a staff attorney with the International Chamber of Commerce, or a professor of law who teaches and writes scholarly articles on cutting-edge issues of the law. One thing is certain: there are as many options out there as there are creative ways of practicing law.

The trick is to examine what interests you in the words *international* and *law*. Is it travel? Is it languages? Is it the complexity of dealing with different legal systems and cultures? Is it human rights? Is it being in an environment where you may be intellectually challenged until you retire or die? Only you know the answer. Once you know what interests you, then you need to find an environment that is conducive to doing what you want to do.

2. In What Type of Environment Do I Want to Practice?

The environment in which you practice can be as important as the type of law you practice. Ask yourself the following questions:

- Do you do well in large bureaucracies, or do you feel that you will scream if someone requires another form to fill out in order to obtain a new hard drive for your computer?

- Do you like small and intimate working environments where you might have to do some photocopying and call your own taxi from time to time, or do you feel claustrophobic and irritated just thinking about it?
- Do you want lots of human contact and consider yourself a people person, or would you rather communicate ?
- Do you like to have an audience (such as in litigation or lecturing), or would you rather hide in a closet?
- Do you like cocktail parties and public relations events, or would you rather spend your evenings researching on the Internet?
- Do you like not knowing what each day will bring, or does the uncertainty bring on an anxiety attack?
- Do you like to travel and are you always prepared to leave town, or do you get stressed and exhausted every time you see a suitcase?

The list can go on and on, but I am sure you get the point. It is not just the intellectual gray matter that counts, but the environment in which you will use your gray matter.

3.   What Are My Lifestyle Choices?

Not all careers will give you choices with regard to where you live and the hours you work. In-house positions can be as time-consuming and stressful as law firm positions. Do not make any assumptions when interviewing and making choices about which position to accept. Being independent can help or hinder, depending on how you organize your life and what type of practice you have.

If you have made certain decisions about lifestyle choices, then you should be very clear about them. For example, I always wanted to have a full-time legal career and had no guilt attacks when juggling work and family, although I did have a lot of headaches and didn't get a manicure very often! Women and men who want to have a full-time career and a family life should be prepared to obtain good and reliable organizational support to manage the stress level for late nights, weekends, and unexpected and prolonged travel.

I had it somewhat easy because French labor laws are very friendly to women who want to work and still have a family. European employers generally tend to be supportive of mothers who work, although your career may take longer to develop if you have a baby a year. In France, paid maternity leave is obligatory for women employees, and it is currently 10 weeks for the first child and increases thereafter per additional child. Moreover, the annual five–six weeks' French vacation can be added to maternity leave, so women can be absent and paid for 15 weeks in the year they give birth. Both men and women can also take parental leaves of absence, although they are not remunerated. Child care is subsidized by the state, and most large urban areas have maternal assistants, nursery schools, and other collective child-care facilities so that you can find child care adapted to your lifestyle and budget.

It also helps to have a supportive—and I mean that in all senses of the word—spouse who is prepared to assume and oversee the household tasks, including the dry cleaning, food shopping, and paying the bills, when the other spouse is traveling, working all night, or just generally exhausted. It also helped having a spouse who had a full-time, dependable position when I started my own firm, as well as a good sense of humor and an ability to see options when I saw none. My husband and I often realized we would both be out of town on business trips with a three-year-old at home and no food in the house. The trick is getting your priorities right and focusing on what is the most important issue during any given crisis—and not losing sight of the fact that this is the life you have chosen.

My advice is that it is all feasible, but you need to be very organized and willing to compromise on how your time is spent and with whom. Most important, you need to be able to be happy with your choices so that you do not spend your days and nights second-guessing yourself and feeling guilty.

H. Lessons Learned

We all have hindsight after the fact and are very good at ignoring and forgetting it. Here are a few lessons that I carry with me to this day.

1. Compromises in Job Choices

If you are going to make them—and please, get over it, everyone makes them—try to be very clear-sighted about what compromises you are making and why you are making them before you make them. (See the previous discussion on lifestyle choices.) If you are not honest with yourself and do not take the time to adequately reflect on and get insight into your motivations, intentions, and expectations, as well as your strengths and weaknesses, you will find yourself frustrated and disappointed. This may take some work on your part, but it is well worth the time and effort, and it should be a continual process to be carried out before, during, and after each choice and change. I spent months deliberating my last change of position, questioning my motives, reasons, advantages, and disadvantages.

2. Manage Expectations

Go easy on yourself. Keep your expectations in line with reality. If you expect too much, you will indeed be disappointed, probably frustrated, and possibly angry. Do not oversell yourself to either yourself or others. It is better for your employer/partner/associates to be happily surprised than unhappily disappointed. Do not let anyone know that you think you are more intelligent than your boss, even if, in fact, you are. Presumptuousness is not a good idea if you are under the age of 50, and even then . . . .

Take the time to take stock of the situation you are in and the one you would like to be in. Are you fulfilled? Satisfied? Are your feelings and expectations and dreams based on reality? Feasible? What do you need to be doing to get where you want to go? Be truthful and frank, and discuss your insights and ideas with those in your close circle of friends and family who know you best. And find and use a mentor.

3. Find Mentors and Join Associations

Do not try to go it alone. I did not have a mentor. No one volunteered, and no one told me that a mentor was an essential part of building a successful career. This was one of my errors, thinking that I could manage without help—assuming I knew where to look for it. Looking back, I am not sure what I could have done to change the lack of mentorship except to have involved myself in professional associations much sooner in my career. Having made this mistake, I have gone out of my way to help others avoid it and have acted and continue to act as a mentor to young and less-young attorneys, many of whom I have met through the ABA Section of International Law.

As a mentor, I have listened to horror stories of gender discrimination against women attorneys, rewritten resumés of friends who wanted to change direction, given doses of reality to Americans who want to practice law in Paris, given advice on how to request and get an increase in remuneration, and distributed networking information over many lunches in Paris. Of course, it helps to live in Paris, since at least you eat and drink well while dispensing advice.

I cannot overemphasize the necessity of finding a mentor. Irrespective of where you are working and what you are doing, find a mentor. A mentor is someone who will help you read and interpret situations and help you keep out of trouble. He or she should be someone you respect who is willing to listen to you and keep your confidences. It's a two-way street: A good mentor is only as good as you allow that person to be. Shop around: Good mentors are not on every doorstep. A few are better than none.

The mentor can be in the organization/company/law firm where you work or outside of it. One excellent place to find supportive mentors is in the ABA, and in particular the International Section, if you are interested in international law. Other types of local, state, and specialized bar associations are also good places to start. If you are in a foreign culture, this can be more daunting, because most cultures are less transparent, frank, and open than American culture. You can always begin with the American associations, including the ABA, in the country where you are residing and then branch out once you understand who the players are.

Never, ever (repeat this daily) make an enemy if you can avoid it. The world is a small place, and the international legal community is even smaller. I have come across acquaintances whom I did not particularly take to when I first met them in Paris 28 years ago, but with whom I became friends and colleagues years later, and with whom I now happily share advice and information.

4. Take What Comes Your Way and Use the Experience to Your Benefit

Unless you can see into the future (in which case you have no business being a lawyer), you will not be able to plan your career 25 years in advance, even if you try. Life is unpredictable, and those who are successful are usually those who know how to make lemonade out of lemons. There is no right career path, and there are rarely any wrong moves. Learn from your mistakes and keep learning.

5. Certain Truths Remain Constant

- *Take your studies seriously.* It is easier to get a solid education when you are young than when you are 50. If you do not learn the trade well, you will not succeed, irrespective of the area of the law in which you intend to practice. The courses that you choose to take in law school should interest you, and you should study hard and learn the skills of a good lawyer: listening, researching, paying attention to detail, writing, and advocating.
- *Be curious and ask questions.* The most intelligent attorneys I know are aware of what they don't know and ask questions. Don't be embarrassed or afraid. You are not expected to know all of the answers, but you are expected to know where and how to find the answers. Be wary of those who claim to know it all.
- *Only idiots do not or cannot change their minds.* If you have made a choice that is not right for you, don't get stuck, and don't be stubborn and remorseful; change directions. And while you are digesting this advice . . .
- *Do not be negative or complain too loudly.* No matter how much you dislike what you are doing, or regret doing it, do not *ever* admit it to anyone other than your closest friends. No one likes someone who whines. The example I like to use to illustrate this point is one of my good friends who could crawl through a field of cow dung while being eaten alive by mosquitoes and regale you with tales of the view and how wonderful it is. As long as you are not fooling yourself, a positive attitude about your current situation will keep your spirits bright and give you the motivation to change.
- *It is easier to downgrade than upgrade.* It is easier to go from a big, well-known firm to a small firm than the inverse. When in doubt, start big and downsize. You do not have to stay big for more than a couple of years, but the experience is great, and it will solidify your credentials.

- *It is easier to make a career move if your contact book is up-to-date.* Keep in contact with old and new acquaintances, friends, and mentors that you have made in the associations and organizations you have joined. This is a full-time job, and it requires attention and work. Do not neglect the benefit of keeping in touch.

- *It is easier and more practical to get diverse experience at the beginning of your career.* Try to get as much different experience as you can in the first three to five years of your career by, for example, rotating departments in the same firm. Realizing after 25 years of real estate practice that you would rather be doing mergers and acquisitions in Italy is good—better late than never—but it is more complicated. By experiencing different types of law and different types of practices, you will learn what you do and do not like in a constructive manner instead of waking up one day and feeling like you have wasted half of your career.

6. Travel and Learn about Different Cultures and Languages

There is nothing more embarrassing and less constructive than American attorneys who assume that their foreign colleagues, clients, and adversaries speak and write in "their" English; eat, drink, and dress in the same manner; and negotiate, draft and sign contracts and agreements; hire and fire employees; litigate, arbitrate, and mediate; and purchase, lease, and sell assets and shares of companies and their goods and services in the same manner as they do.

It might sound trite, but any lawyer practicing in the international arena must have some sensitivity to different cultures and languages. Yes, it is helpful to learn a second and third language, if for no other reason than to know what it means not to understand and to feel vulnerable and somewhat helpless. It is a well-earned lesson in humility, which is necessary when traveling and negotiating in languages and cultures other than the one in which we were brought up. And this advice includes the United Kingdom, Australia, Canada, and other English-speaking countries.

Verbal communication and body language is crucial. Assume you know nothing about the foreign culture, even if you think you do. A little knowledge can be dangerous, both personally and professionally. Read as much as you can, including novels by national authors, and ask as many questions as you feel is appropriate. Blissful ignorance does not exist in international law. Living and working outside the United States in whatever capacity is always a fruitful experience. My credo is: "Look, listen, and learn."

I. Conclusion

I have attempted to share my insights into my own career and draw certain conclusions from them, which I hope will be useful to you. Undoubtedly, you will have your own experiences and will draw your own conclusions

There are many things I wish I had known before I started my career: I wish I had known that I needed a mentor; I wish someone had told me that networking is essential; I wish I had joined the International Section of the ABA before I turned 40. And I wish I had been able to read this book!

Know that there is no secret gate or password to become an international lawyer. Become a good lawyer first, and focus on what interests you. Maintain an open mind about job opportunities, know yourself, and keep a sense of humor and perspective about your life and career. The rest is, as we used to say, "a piece of cake"!

The Road to an International In-House Legal Career

2

by Janet B. Wright and Carolyn Herzog

A. Introduction

We approached writing this chapter with the knowledge that we had ended up in similar places, having followed different paths and starting with only three key factors in common: (1) we are both women; (2) we are both lawyers; and (3) we both share an interest in international practice. Where Carolyn began as a legal generalist with subject-matter expertise and moved into more specific areas of legal expertise, Janet began her career focusing on a legal area of expertise that lent itself to a broader area of practice. In this chapter, we discuss not only how and why we arrived at our current roles, but also how we work to support the evolving definition of global counsel, the key factors for success, and considerations for any person contemplating a move to in-house work in an international environment.

B. How Did We Get Here and Why Do We Stay?

First and foremost, we agree that we are in our current positions because we work with great people, we have interesting challenges to tackle, our careers continue to develop, and we have a global focus that keeps us interested and engaged. What each of us does today represents an evolution from where we started—in part planned, in part as a result of a changing business environment. Being flexible and prepared to take on new challenges is important to your long-term success in an in-house environment.

Janet: I spent 10 years in law firms doing tax and corporate work, including corporate transactions, mergers and acquisitions (M&A), international tax planning, tax litigation, and partnership investments. Having spent five years each at two large law firms, I was ready for a change. I took an in-house position as tax counsel at Dell, focusing on international tax planning for expansions in Asia and Latin America. I then moved to a corporate counsel position and did everything from securities work to global equity compensation compliance to medical privacy compliance. Following that, I led teams that supported Dell's U.S. Consumer and Small Business sales segments, along with their global customer contact centers. I now lead the corporate legal team.

I am responsible for Dell's corporate securities, corporate finance, corporate governance, and general corporate matters. as well as legal department administration. I have found that the work is more challenging in-house, and I thoroughly enjoy being part of a management team. For me, an in-house practice has been more professionally and personally rewarding than my experience at law firms.

Carolyn: My path to an in-house position was much different from Janet's, although my reasoning was much the same. Before law school, I worked in international development at The World Bank. Having studied French, I used my language skills in a francophone African division. I loved it, but knew that I wanted return to school to get a graduate degree in either law or business. Even after deciding to go to law school, I knew that my primary focus was in international practice, and not necessarily a traditional legal practice. Fortunately, I found ways to study and work overseas during law school. After graduating, I again worked in international development, but this time from a legal perspective and in a nonprofit organization. I moved into my first in-house position directly from the nonprofit, which was perhaps a more unusual step at the time than it is today.

I joined AXENT Technologies, Inc. as the third lawyer and as a generalist, doing just about everything that a corporate attorney does in an international, publicly traded company. As the company grew, so did my responsibilities, until I was finally acting as general counsel when the company was acquired by Symantec Corporation in December 2000. Technology is a fast-paced and dynamic environment that can offer in-house counsel a varied area of practice, provided you are eager and willing to dive in even where your background may not lend itself to a current business need. By being flexible and willing to take risks, you may find that your time in-house at a technology company could be a few years or, as in my case, many years with the same company.

My roles have changed significantly as the company has grown and changed: I have been responsible for intellectual property portfolios and asset management, revenue-generating transactions, human resources and employment matters, M&A and related integration, corporate, procurement, compliance, and even real estate. In the past 15 years, I moved from being a general counsel to a business unit head of legal and currently to a regional role as head of legal for Europe, the Middle East, and Africa, which included a move from Washington, D.C. to London nearly four years ago. The initial generalist approach has prepared me well for all my roles, as I am able to spot issues in a general counsel capacity and to enable more effective results by relying on other specialists within our organization and through external networks. Managing a team of nearly 30 people across a broad geography with diverse legal jurisdictions has forced me to accept more ambiguity when the risks are lower, to realize that the right answer is not always intuitive to a U.S. attorney working overseas, and that networking among your peers and finding the right outside counsel to build relationships is critical.

C. Some Thoughts to Consider on Your Path to In-House

Our paths are a good demonstration that there is no one way to establish an international in-house legal career. Where Carolyn began a career in international development, with an interest in several specialties but no primary legal focus, Janet had developed a very specific skill set. Carolyn worked in international organizations and nonprofits before going in-house to a technology company, while Janet established her expertise in a law firm. Certainly, the path from law firm to in-house is the more traditional route, but many factors can help you and an employer decide if you are the right fit.

So what can you do now to start preparing? Before law school, a focus on languages or international studies or a degree with an international interest is a good start. Depending on your career focus, a language skill may be a driving factor. Although French, German, and Spanish are the most widely spoken languages, in today's market, knowing Arabic, Mandarin, or Japanese may create unique opportunities. You may also consider where you want to study. Exchange programs from U.S. universities are great opportunities to immerse yourself in a different culture and to practice language skills. In her third year, Carolyn arranged to do an exchange with a student at the University of Paris law school. It was a challenge, but it posed unique opportunities as well. Being fully immersed into the French law school, she learned about not only the French legal system but also the process of learning, impressions of French and other foreign law students, and how to take oral exams in French. It was daunting at times, but a rewarding experience overall.

If you are considering law school outside the United States, you will find advantages and disadvantages. Many schools outside of the United States are less expensive, but you will likely want to consider obtaining an LL.M. from a well-known U.S. university afterward. You may also consider the reverse scenario, obtaining a J.D. from a U.S. school and doing some post-J.D. studies at a foreign school. Bar reciprocity is something that you should consider, whether you want to practice in or outside the United States or in several countries. Depending on where you work and what you do, the definition of practicing law may vary, and representation may not require local qualification. This is particularly true of in-house work.

If you are practicing now, remember that the very best in-house lawyers working on international legal topics all started out as good lawyers. Whether they have an expertise that they apply globally or an international background that they apply to legal work, they are all fundamentally very good lawyers who spent time finding a job where they could sell those great skills in exchange for the opportunity to work in a global role.

D. Plan or Chance?

Just as you can take numerous paths to forge your career in international in-house practice, you must also have a reasonable amount of flexibility to seize opportunities as they are presented to you. A well-planned career may not always allow you to keep your eyes and mind open to new opportunities, just as lack of planning and focus may not bring you to a point where opportunities are presented at all.

> **Carolyn:** Prior to law school, I held a second job as a self-employed personal career hunter; I spent countless hours researching international careers and weighing my options. At the current point in my career, I can safely say that my professional development has been a healthy combination of planning, sustained enthusiasm, genuine interest in my chosen path, and being in the right place at the right time. It's not about relying on chance, but rather being a reliable, interested, and engaged person so that opportunities come your way first. An in-house career is built on commercial and legal relationships and not on a big ego.
>
> To get the best projects, you first have to be willing to take the less-glamorous assignments and to use your time wisely. There is a common notion that in-house work is a 9-to-5 proposition, in contrast to the long hours required at the larger law firms. While in-house counsel is more rarely presented with a weekend-consuming project at 5 P.M. on a Friday afternoon than your typical first-year law firm associate, you should not expect to succeed by clock-watching.

I know very few in-house leaders who proceeded in their careers by working a 40-hour week. Despite those extra hours, you won't have the luxury of time to spend hours researching the most thorough and safest answer; most often, you will have to make a quick judgment call based on the best available information at the time. This willingness to participate in the analysis and assumption of risk is the key to being seen as a businessperson's lawyer.

In addition to hard work, focus, and flexibility, it's also extremely important to understand how you best fit into a global working environment. Being comfortable among your legal and business colleagues and being able to enjoy your work can become key factors in your career path decisions.

In a constantly changing environment, there are both opportunities and challenges, and longevity in any organization requires fairly regular evaluation of the environment and how we add value to the current and predicted needs of the organization. I haven't always felt in sync with the changes of the moment, and it has, at times, taken great effort and a proactive approach to overcome hurdles and to steer my career in a way that was both rewarding to me and useful to the company.

Janet: The key here is to know yourself. If you like change and want to do a variety of legal work, seek it out. If you like being the expert in a single area of law, do that. Either route can lead to an international scope of responsibility.

My career has been more about chance than planning. At the beginning, I focused on becoming a single-subject expert in tax law. I thought that I would stay in that area of law and never stray. But one thing I discovered about myself is that I really like change and the challenge of the unknown. If you are that way too, stay open to unexpected possibilities and be prepared to take on an area of the law you have never encountered. For example, while working on the corporate legal team at Dell, I was offered a job as the lead lawyer for a sales segment. I didn't hesitate for long before I took the role, even though I had to make the decision without knowing which sales segment it would be and had no expertise in the relevant law. I enjoyed the challenge and learned a great deal, and when I moved back to a role in corporate, the broad commercial experience made me a better corporate lawyer.

Though I have taken more of a generalist route, I have colleagues who are subject matter experts with global roles in litigation, intellectual property, and employee benefits. So if you are passionate about a single subject, you can build your expertise and then leverage it into a global area of responsibility.

As you think through the generalist-versus-expert question, you should consider the type of legal department you are joining. If you are one of three or four lawyers, be prepared to spend one day doing litigation, one day working on the company proxy statement, and the next day negotiating a software license. If you like variety and the challenge of something new, you will enjoy a smaller department. Larger departments have generalist jobs too, but they also tend to house specialists who spend all of their time solely in their area of expertise. If you are a specialist and want to stay that way, look at larger departments.

E. Thoughts on Finding the Right Fit for You

While the following considerations are certainly not all that you might consider in making the decision to join a global company's legal department, they are at least a starting point from which you can ask additional questions.

If you are considering going in-house, do your research well. Consider whether size, industry, location of headquarters, and current international practice are important to you. We all have different priorities, and you should follow your interests in selecting the right environment for you. Consider your end goals and where you will have the most enjoyable experience. The work in a $100-million company is not less interesting or less complex than in a $100-billion company. If you are interested in being the general counsel at a younger age, a smaller company will offer you that opportunity sooner than a larger company, where you will no doubt have greater opportunity to learn from more experienced leaders.

Janet: Once you identify a company in which you are interested, find out everything you can about the company, its business, and the relevant industry. Review the company's securities filings in detail, as they tell you a lot about the company's business as well as the industry. If you can, talk to lawyers who have worked in, for, or with the legal department as well. And get as much information as you can when you interview. Questions you should ask include:

- What is the structure of the legal department, and where does the department fit into the company structure? Does the general counsel report to the CEO?
- How is the department viewed by others in the business? Does legal have a seat at the table with the business team, or is it viewed as an adversary?
- What is the relationship between the department and the board? Does the general counsel attend board meetings?
- What are the expectations for the role?
- How will you know in one year whether you have been successful?
- How do members of the legal team view their clients? Do they talk about them as colleagues and partners or as adversaries?
- How do the lawyers in the department view each other? Are there legal teams for different divisions, and do they work together or do they compete?
- If you are a specialist, how high up is the most senior specialist in your area? Does she report to the general counsel? Is she the general counsel? Or is she five levels down from the general counsel? Wherever she is, is that a job to which you would aspire?
- Does the legal department encourage developing relationships with colleagues at other companies?
- How does the department focus on professional development? Are outside learning opportunities encouraged? Do lawyers rotate though various roles in the department? Are mentors common or rare?

Carolyn: I recommend to anyone looking at a change to move in-house, or, in seeking opportunities that will expand international exposure, to truly explore the environment, including current job descriptions and informational interviews of similarly situated counsel. Are careers built on a generalist approach that is regionally focused or on specialist positions that are globally applied? I have a great sense of accomplishment and contribution in my role, but I have had to work extremely hard and diplomatically to gain trust. I pride myself on being responsive and sincere in anything that I do—lack of availability and personal accountability are not attributes that fit well in an in-house team.

Where you are in your career may play a big part in your selection of the right department for your current needs, which may include getting some management experience, working overseas, or even experimenting in a business role. Naturally, lifestyle, location, salary, stability of the industry, or dynamic mobility may all be factors. For me, having fun and working with people that I respect and enjoy is just as important as having interesting work and a management structure that enables me to do my best work.

The fact that the company I work for is willing to discuss the work-family balance is important to me. I work extremely hard, but I also have many life interests and know that it is easier for me to keep my staff engaged if they also realize that the company offers reasonable flexibility to enable important lifestyle choices. The choice is always a personal one, and a sense of commitment will also always be evident to management, but time to focus on things other than work also lend creativity and perspective to the work environment.

F. Building International Legal and Business Partner Relationships

Once you find the right job, in order to succeed in a multinational environment, you must be accessible and globally aware. The purpose of global business is to create access and opportunity, and this theme should carry through to your approach as in-house counsel.

Carolyn: By creating access and opportunity, there is a greater give-and-take, rather than a sense that your gain is at the expense of others. Particularly in a U.S.-based company, there can be great sensitivity to the roles at headquarters as compared to the roles in other regions. A successful international career requires an ability to understand and adjust to different work and cultural environments. If you are viewed as applying your country's ideals and expectations to foreign settings, you will not fit in, and you will not be given the access that you desire. This sensitivity should extend to in-country or in-region variations.

Colleagues in certain international regions may be working alone, whereas those in the United States or the headquarters of an overseas office often have the benefit of a team environment. Whether alone or in smaller groups, lawyers outside of headquarters may feel disconnected from the goals of the department and may have closer relationships with their business colleagues in the region. In some cases, it can be difficult to get the infirmation you need on a global basis to truly be effective. This is where prioritization and global awareness are key elements to your success.

You will have to focus your priorities on the greatest needs of your business and rely on regional and specialist resources to help you. You must recognize and appreciate that your regional counsel has the responsibility to support the needs of all the business in his or her respective territories and will not have endless resources to answer every question you might have on how a particular area of law is handled in Australia, Spain, or Saudi Arabia. By helping your regional partners understand the needs of your business and finding ways to make their jobs easier, you will forge better relationships and derive greater value from those relationships over time.

I have found that by creating more efficient ways to share information (i.e., through online resources, training, and playbooks), I help my colleagues save time, provide better answers, and give me more targeted and valuable input.

Janet: If you work for a company with locations around the globe, your ability to build relationships with colleagues with whom you do not share a common first language or a culture will be the key to your success. You must have exceptionally good relationship skills that can work remotely, and you must be sensitive to other cultures and ways of doing business.

Here are a few steps for connecting with your colleagues: First, find out who you need to know—ask your manager for names of colleagues and clients you need to meet. Second, set up a meeting or call with those people; tell them who you are and what you do, and ask them about their area of responsibility. Third, take any opportunity you can to meet people face-to-face. Travel to see them, and make sure that when they are in your office, you have time to meet with them. Finally, always keep your commitments; if you don't become the person your international colleagues and clients can rely on, you will not be able to succeed in a multinational company.

Two things in particular have worked for me in developing working relationships with my colleagues and understanding the many laws that impact any given project. First, I regularly spend time on the phone with my international colleagues without a specific agenda—we talk about work, projects that are under way, trends we see in the business, and our families. That kind of contact helps us get ahead of issues. Second, we have subject-matter calls across the department: we have a monthly call for all the lawyers involved in privacy compliance, another for all lawyers who support the services business, one for all lawyers doing employment work, and so on. It's a great way to share information, learn something, and build a sense that we are a global team.

G. Challenges in Networking Outside of Your Company

One of the potential disappointments to career law firm lawyers who move in-house is the lack of funding and interest in sending counsel to meetings and networking opportunities. It's simply not a priority for in-house counsel to spend time networking outside of the company, and there is not the same level of funding to attend such events. This doesn't mean, however, that we should ignore the importance of networking.

Networking while in-house has to be a priority. When you no longer have to develop business, it's easy to neglect your network. But your network is how you will find people at other companies who can help you with answering legal questions, navigating in-house politics, keeping current on your industry, and perhaps finding your next job. Your biggest challenge will be making yourself get up from your very busy desk and take the time to network.

Start by using the networks that are easily available to you. Join the ABA and participate in relevant sections. If you work for a multinational, we recommend the Section of International Law, because you will find lawyers doing many different types of work around the globe. A local Association of Corporate Counsel chapter is also a good resource, as is your local bar or local networking groups. Don't forget that your company is a corporate citizen—you will also be able to take advantage of networking with businesspeople in your community via volunteerism, chambers of commerce, and community service.

H.   Things to Consider in Business Unit Management

Carolyn: I've seen many lawyers come to work in-house and become overly concerned with title and stature or with the ever-elusive glorifying project. Merely finding a job in-house will not make you an insider, and being a trusted business partner is not contingent upon title position or how much experience you have, either external or internal to the company.

Just as with any relationship, you have to develop a level of trust and earn the confidence of your colleagues, both within the legal department and within the business units that you support. Unfortunately, people come to the job with their own biases and expectations, and we often have to prove ourselves repeatedly. Find ways to be invited to meetings by showing interest in the subject matter and offering your thoughts, whether they are legal in nature or business-oriented.

Remember that being a good in-house lawyer requires your understanding of the business goals. To add the best value, I firmly believe that corporate counsel should be an integral part of the business team at all levels. A true go-to lawyer understands and empathizes with the business needs and can offer business-solution-oriented advice on the legal requirements to enable those needs appropriately. The company's executives have to be able to rely on us to enable the business within responsible legal parameters. We must guide the process and create confidence in our leaders.

You will encounter executives who just want to hear "yes" and for you to provide the proverbial rubber stamp. This is not the kind of value-added service that I would advocate, and it certainly does not enable you to gain respect and confidence. On rare occasions I need to say "no" as an absolute, but most of the time I try to find a way to achieve objectives responsibly. When I do need to draw a more stringent line, I make sure to do this by first expressing my understanding of the situation and then by explaining why certain objectives are not attainable. Being a good business lawyer and demonstrating excellent judgment also means applying the right level of risk to your decisions.

At the same time, a purely business focus could lead you to a point where you are not thinking as a lawyer. It's equally important to keep up with the law and the practice of law in-house. Not only does a good corporate counsel need to understand the law, but he or she must also foresee the trends in how to communicate and interpret the practice of that law. This is often the hardest skill to teach. Each company has its own risk personality, which often changes over time. The legal department is a key to the pulse of any company's risk profile. Being a part of the business team and balancing risk means that we can't play it 100 percent safe all the time, but we should demonstrate an ability to take risks with our business partners.

Developing your own personal style is important, because it will allow you to be yourself and feel comfortable in doing what is necessary to get the job done. It's taken me years to develop and understand my own personal style. I've been accused of being both a tough woman and too nice. I think it's often harder for women to become comfortable with their business style: What is the appropriate level of push-back? How confidently should we behave? My personal belief is that you should be true to your own personality. I don't try to be someone different at work than I am in my personal life, with the exception of a level of professionalism and appropriate formality.

Janet: For an in-house lawyer, "just say no" is not the motto. A successful in-house lawyer is part of a business management team that consists of a CEO or division manager, a finance manager, a controller, a sales leader or other business expert, a lawyer, and so on. As part of that team, the lawyer must understand the company's plans and goals, its industry landscape, its customer needs, and its appetite for risk, and must work as part of a team executing a plan in the most profitable, most cost-advantaged manner. Legal compliance is a must, but thereafter legal issues—whether, for example, local law would allow a target company's suppliers to cancel their contracts after an acquisition—are some of the risks that must be balanced against the opportunities. Most of the lawyer's time is not spent deciding whether a course of action is legal; instead, the focus is risk assessment and risk mitigation. You must be able to quickly evaluate how much risk flows from the actions that implement the strategic plan, whether that risk can be decreased without detracting from the business goal, and whether achieving the goal is worth the remaining inherent risk.

If you are beginning to envision a tightrope walk, you are getting the picture. You must have good business judgment and be able to work as part of a management team, but you must also be able to think independently and, when necessary, either find another, less risky way to accomplish the team's goal or, in some cases, be willing to say "no" while trying to maintain your status as a respected business partner and avoid becoming the dreaded "sales prevention team."

I.   Managing Other Lawyers

Good lawyers can make great managers, but management is not taught in law school and often does not come naturally for lawyers. Finding a strong manager and being part of a talented management team can make all the difference to your in-house experience.

Carolyn: In-house departments tend not to have a structure in place that encourages discussion of career development and morale. It is often assumed that lawyers are so grateful to move in-house from the stereotypical work-farm attitude in a law firm that management sometimes forgets about key factors for development and retention of staff. It's easy to lose sight of the reality that an engaged, happy, and motivated workforce does a better job and makes the jobs of others easier.

I have found that there is ample opportunity in an in-house environment to influence how management can improve focus on its employees. As professionals, lawyers value education and development as well as recognition for the successful outcomes that arise from innovation and hard work. I have also realized that people can develop as subject matter experts and as managers with a broader range of general expertise. As a team grows, so do the requirements of a manger to balance focus on staff development and engagement with individual projects. As founder and chair of the department's Development Committee, I now invest extra time in creating programs to train staff and to institute standards for development. I also make sure that we have time to team-build in new and fun ways—this may be through skills-related, knowledge-sharing, or community outreach activities, or it may be simply finding casual opportunities for local team engagement.

Proactive engagement may also require conflict management skills. When conflicts arise among team members or between team members and business partners, managers need to step in to help resolve differences and grow relationships. I need my staff not only to trust me, but also to trust and rely on their colleagues so that I am not a one-stop shop for information and approvals. By relying more on each other, we are also a more creative and productive team.

It is also important to recognize and reward other leaders on the team and to create opportunities for individuals to shine. Over time, I have learned to recognize the strengths and areas for potential development of staff so that I can help them excel where they are strongest and to develop where they have room to grow. Managing your staff is not enough; leaders today need to lead outward and upward. Think beyond the parameters of the legal department and reach out to colleagues in other regions and other business units.

Good management includes some of the networking that was discussed earlier. It also means letting go, or, in other words, that all-powerful corporate term "delegation." As independent professionals, we can often see delegation as "passing the buck" or not doing all that our job requires. We can forget that delegation gives others a chance to learn and develop, while giving managers more time to focus on developing others and ourselves. Consider doing what I did many years ago—by taking an extended vacation after much planning and preparing, I succumbed to the humble reality that the company could go on without me. By doing so, I created an opportunity for other team members to step up to new experiences. And miraculously, rather than proving myself unnecessary, I returned to a stronger and more capable team and was asked to step up to a new role myself. Now, granted, it takes a special kind of trust in your own management to have this kind of result. Still, I found it interesting that, rather than creating an impression that I had lost focus and commitment, I returned fully committed and received compliments from my colleagues for being a strong manager and leader in creating opportunities for others.

Janet: It's fairly rare in a law firm to have a manager, but you do have a lot of bosses. Partners who give you work, your department head, your mentors, and your clients. In-house you will have a manager and you may also become a manager, both of which require skills that law firms will not teach you. But if you want to succeed in-house, you have to become a good manager who can build a solid team.

I have a lot of responsibilities to my team. It's my job to assist each of them with legal issues they are working on, help them develop into better lawyers, make sure they are not working too hard but also have enough work, keep them on track with their projects, ensure that performance and development plans are in place and that we take the time to act on them, challenge them to be both independent thinkers and good busi-

ness partners, and act as a navigator through the myriad politics of the corporation. I also have responsibilities to my manager. It's critical that I build a solid and diverse team and that
we manage the work well, balance risk appropriately, succeed
as trusted advisors to our clients, and ensure that the General
Counsel is well informed on key issues and projects.

Building and managing a great team can be one of the most
satisfying parts of an in-house career, but you should not approach it as an easy task for which you are well-prepared. Watch
the good managers in your organization, study their habits,
work for them if you can, and ask one of them to mentor you.

J. Selecting and Managing Outside Counsel

The basics always ring true: find a counsel who is responsive, understands your business, doesn't try to go around you, and offers sage,
business-friendly, current, and accurate advice.

Janet: Outside counsel can be your greatest asset, but they can
also be a huge headache. Select the right outside counsel for
what you need done, make sure they understand that you are
the client and you are in control, and then manage them closely.

You might be looking for outside counsel for a variety of
reasons. Maybe you simply need local counsel in a country in
which you do not have a lawyer. Or you might be looking for
specific expertise. You might be under-resourced and need to
send out your overflow. Hire to fit the need, whether that is a
well-known global expert in the field or just a solid business
lawyer from around the corner to get a contract done. Find out
what your company's policies are. Do you have the authority
to hire outside counsel? Do you get to choose, or must you
hire from an approved list? Are there particular outside counsel who have already earned the respect and trust of your new
colleagues?

Once you find the right lawyer for your needs, negotiate
costs and set expectations. You need to plan your budget, so
you must know what a project will cost. Your outside counsel
should understand the business, your goal for the project, and

how to communicate appropriately with you or, in some circumstances, with your client. There are few things worse than an outside counsel who goes around you and gives an answer directly to the internal client without understanding or being able to explain the business implications that flow from that answer, losing credibility for both of you.

Carolyn: In addition to the criteria already discussed, in a multinational company you must also consider the international savvy of your individual counsel or the firm and the consistency of their advice. Just because you are comfortable with the counsel you use in San Diego doesn't mean that their colleague in London has the same style and reliability. Look at where your business is growing and consider in advance what regional needs you may have, including interpretation of law and translation services. Prepare for your resourcing needs and anticipate costs—outside counsel is a big part of the annual budgeting considerations for a legal department.

It's important to set expectations and to understand your company's direction with respect to legal costs: Is the company prepared to invest in more permanent in-house counsel (and it is your job to advise them if you think it's appropriate), or are the current issues temporary and best allocated to outside counsel? Overflow costs should be budgeted and planned for—otherwise, you risk either giving up your life by working nights and weekends or giving up your reputation by not being able to manage your work effectively. The reserves for legal costs associated with big-ticket items such as litigation and M&A are all part of the general counsel's planning process. In some companies, these costs are not part of the legal budget but are allocated to specific cost centers.

In managing outside counsel, it's important to be clear in your communications by stating not only what you want, but also what you *don't* want. Outside counsel will try to be thorough and will usually set expectations on time and cost, but it is your responsibility to manage this process. Depending on your regular needs, you may choose one counsel upon whom you rely exclusively. In other areas, you may decide that a little competition is the best way to keep costs down and information current. You should also consider what other factors are important to you and your company beyond cost and reliability (and discuss with your management as needed), such as global offices or affiliations, diversity, and even personality (is the firm too formal for your company?).

Along with cost, I'll freely admit that I welcome a free gift with purchase. I appreciate an outside counsel who anticipates my needs, not just by shopping opportunities to their colleagues (e.g., "I see that you've been sued for trademark infringement in Lithuania, and I'd like to introduce you to my colleague."), but also by anticipating my needs in the business context (e.g., providing me with a template form or a summary of a new law). A counsel who is in tune with your company and its competitors and who is interested in helping you provide superior legal service is going to preserve a longer-term relationship.

K. Specialization: Benefit or Barrier to Promotion?

There are many different theories on the best way to gain access to the most-coveted in-house positions or to develop a career that will lead you to a general counsel position. By now, you should recognize our theory that many paths can lead you to your goal. The question of whether to specialize and, from there, in which topics to specialize is an individual choice, and your ability to move in different directions is not always dependent on your specialization.

> **Carolyn:** I developed my career more as a generalist and it has suited me well so far, but there are many times when I thought that a specialization would have benefited my career. Because of my interest in an international practice, certain topics lend themselves to a multinational business setting, including corporate law, tax, intellectual property, or litigation (particularly if you have experience managing cross-regional disputes). Depending on your particular strategy, your career development choices may vary.

If, for instance, you want to go in-house and you currently specialize in employment law, then you might want to seek opportunities to diversify your experiences. If you think that you eventually want to move out of law and into a business role, this may also impact your decisions. I know an employment law specialist who moved from an in-house legal position to the head of human resources, and I know a tax lawyer who is now responsible for international M&A.

There are endless examples of exceptions to the rules, and your choices should follow your goals. If you have a specialty that you are committed to and one for which there is an ongoing need, there is no reason why you shouldn't enjoy a healthy career in that area. If, however, you want to manage a staff with broader responsibilities, then it will be important to find opportunities to expand your experience. The opposite is also true: if you have built a career on good legal sense applied to a variety of situations, you will rely on outside counsel in a different way for more specialized tasks, and if you want to be a general counsel, then you should consider deepening your experience in specialized areas, such as litigation management, asset management (including intellectual property), corporate law, and M&A.

Janet: Specialization is not a barrier to promotion, but, depending on the company, it can be a barrier to becoming general counsel. That is not always true, but if you are a specialist and you want to stay that way, it's generally a good idea to look for a larger company with a larger department. Find out how high the specialists in that department go. Is the general counsel a specialist? Are her direct reports specialists? Can a specialist become a vice president, or is the lead trademark or real estate or ERISA lawyer, for example, a senior counsel? Make sure that the specialists in that company have levels of responsibility and are working on projects that fit with your career goals.

L.   A Few Things You Should Know if You Want to Be General Counsel

We'll start with the reality check again: there is the general counsel who graduated from law school last year and is helping his buddy with a start-up venture, and then there is the general counsel who seemingly speaks as though she has taken presentation skills training from Charlton Heston—if she says it, it must be true. Regardless of tenure or charisma, all general counsels today will be presented with different challenges than their predecessors had, with increased scrutiny on compliance, economic pressures to do more with less—and faster, and growing teams that have the evolutionary business-savvy skills required of in-house counsel. Naturally, the challenges and considerations are vastly different for management of a small, privately held company than those of a large publicly traded company, and we cannot hope to cover them all.

> **Janet:** The most respected general counsels are usually exceptional people. They have great leadership abilities and outstanding business judgment, are great strategists, communicate very well, have executive presence, tend to be very calm even in the face of calamity, think creatively about law department management, inspire their teams, and have an uncanny knack for convincing people that spending time and money on compliance and governance is of utmost importance. They don't wait for problems to appear; they learn the business, anticipate the problems, and then avoid them. Like chess masters, it is second nature for them to quickly analyze the business ramifications of a legal decision. They also tend to be people who are in the right place at the right time, either by luck or exceptionally careful planning.
>
> If you want to be a general counsel, you should get as much experience as you can through practice, practice, practice. Find a great mentor and try to work for a great general counsel. Focus on developing all the skills you will need, including outstanding business judgment and strategic agility.
>
> **Carolyn:** In many ways, the general counsel is the ultimate go-to lawyer and the ultimate leader. The general counsel must

understand the business at the highest levels and have the ability to develop and lead staff who can aid the prioritization of legal requirements and business needs, the growth and enablement of company priorities, and a vision for the department as it fits within the company. A general counsel can be seen as a visionary and the ultimate judge to determine the values, level of risk assumption, and even the personality and influence of the legal department. The general counsel sees the CEO, the board of directors, and, if public, the company's shareholders as his or her primary client.

While the various divisions of any company will surely have competing priorities and demands, the general counsel must decide how to allocate legal resources to best enable the business. In a publicly traded company, the general counsel will usually be the authority to present to the board of directors and to be accountable to the public and governmental authorities on matters of compliance. The general counsel is not only an advocate for the company, but is also the voice representing its ethical obligations. In the post-Sarbanes-Oxley world, and in the wake of scandal and subsequent regulation worldwide, the general counsel has an even bigger and more important role to balance the ethical, purely legal, and business advisory responsibilities.

If you want to be a general counsel, you will need to follow many of the principles outlined in this chapter: understand your business, manage a responsible and insightful budget, create key relationships both internally and externally, keep current with the law, be a go-to lawyer, master your role as risk manager, have a vision, achieve balance, and lead an exceptional staff with reliable and talented outside counsel. Easy enough, right?

M. Conclusion

Many roads can lead to a successful career as in-house counsel for a multinational company. The path you follow will be unique, and we hope that the advice in this chapter will help you make key choices along the way. Certainly, many factors will influence your direction.

The key is not in knowing exactly what you require every step of the way, but in focusing on smaller goals and, if you know your ultimate goal, setting a flexible strategy to help you make important decisions.

You may find, as we have, that your direction and goals may change as you gain exposure to new areas. We hope you will find the road less traveled to be an adventure well worth pursuing and the opportunities vast and exciting.

Demystifying the Career of an International Derivatives Lawyer

3

by Jeffrey B. Golden

A. Introduction

What an exciting time to be contemplating a career in international law! In private practice, it was not always like this. Thirty-five years ago, interviewing for an associate's position with the leading Wall Street firms, I had to apologize for my interest in international law. Senior partners at the firms that I visited denied the relevance of international law and practice. However, all that has changed. International is where it's at. These days, the law firms on Wall Street, like elsewhere, are determined to convince recruits that their practices on offer are truly international.

The choices and opportunities certainly seemed more limited when I graduated from law school. I joined New York law firm Cravath, Swaine & Moore, which at least showed two overseas branch offices on its letterhead. When, after five years in the New York office, I was offered a posting to London, I grabbed it. My wife is English, and we were thrilled. Not everyone thought this was a career-enhancing move, however. Another associate queried the logic of my transferring to what he described as an outpost. I replied that the senior partner had assured me that the plan was to expand the London office, but my colleague was unconvinced. "What are they going to do?" he asked. "Add another Rapifax machine?"

In fact, with my arrival in London, the size of the Cravath office there was increased by 50 percent—from two to three lawyers. In an office that size, it was probably inevitable that I would be stretched by a broad range of transactional experience, including, in this case, capital markets, banking, general corporate, joint venture, and, especially, merger and acquisition work. Looking back, that stretching was not an altogether bad thing.

In the early 1980s, our client, Salomon Brothers, came to us seeking documentation and legal advice in connection with a new financial product—a swap—which derived its value from movements in prices in underlying interest rate and currency markets. There was not much competition among our colleagues for this novel work, out of the Cravath mainstream as it was ("If it is important, we would already be doing it"), but Dan Cunningham, then a partner in the Cravath New York office (and later my partner at Allen & Overy LLP), and I were fascinated by the opportunity and the dynamic investment bankers we were mixing with in this fledgling market. Maybe it was the Concorde flights. Because very few lawyers understood the business, those of us who did were being flown back and forth between New York and London on very fast airplanes. Deadlines were tight, but the substantial margins for these deals in the early days of the business allowed for some serious celebrations when the deadlines were met and the deals closed.

However, different lawyers in different rooms and at different times had produced different forms of swap agreements for their respective banks, and the conflicts these gave rise to and the costs of the lengthy negotiations that followed were a real impediment to the growth of the business. To avoid a "battle of the forms," Dan and I were asked by Salomon Brothers and other leading market participants to attempt to harmonize the various agreement precedents then being used. The code of contract terms that we produced and the master agreement that followed from it became the industry's standard. We continued in the years that followed to advise the International Swaps and Derivatives Association (ISDA) in the development of the ISDA Master Agreement, including the most recently published version of that document, and I am told that ISDA Master Agreements now support more than

$600 trillion notional amount trading today. So I hope that we got the contract right!

The law students whom I interview sometimes ask me, "How was it, when you were a 2L, that you knew you wanted to pursue a career in derivatives or the law of finance?" Well, as you can see, I did not and, in the case of derivatives, could not know, since the underlying business had not yet been invented. In fact, I did not have much of an idea what lay ahead or what were the distinguishing features of the practices of lawyers in big law firms. When I turned up for my first day at Cravath, a stern lady came out of the personnel office and confronted me with the question, "Which department, corporate or litigation?" "Which one is the IBM case?" I asked. "That's litigation," she replied. "Right," I said. "I'll take corporate." And my whole career followed from that.

In any event, after more than 15 years at Cravath and 10 years into what was meant to be an 18-month stint in the Cravath London office, I had come to know well, through my M&A and derivatives work, the leading so-called Magic Circle English law practices. When the rules that had prevented English law qualified solicitors from partnering with non-English law qualified lawyers were relaxed, one of these firms, Allen & Overy, got brave and decided to put together an English and U.S. law capability under one roof. A&O approached me and asked if I would come across the street, join them as their first non-English law qualified partner, and start up the firm's U.S. law practice. The lure of taking that road less traveled was irresistible. That was 1994. Where does the time go?

The Allen & Overy U.S. Law Group that I remember consisting of one lawyer sitting in London—the only non-English law qualified partner—is now a diversified global U.S. law practice, which last I heard has more than 300 U.S. law qualified lawyers, in a firm with more lawyers outside the United Kingdom than in it and more non-English law qualified partners than English law qualified ones. Approximately 2,500 lawyers overall are practicing out of 30 countries literally around the globe. My partners at the firm included (in addition to British and Americans) French, German, Dutch, Spanish, Italian, Polish, Russian, Chinese, and Japanese lawyers. A lot has changed in the past decade. Why wasn't this on offer when I came out of law school?

Another thing that has changed is where I now work. When I joined Allen & Overy, it was written in the partnership deeds that a partner would automatically retire on reaching the age of 60.[1] Fortunately, "old" is an acceptable complement for professorial duties, and I was delighted when, following my retirement from A&O, my alma mater, The London School of Economics and Political Science, invited me to join the LSE's law faculty as Visiting Professor to teach financial markets law and regulation and the relevance of both to sustainable development.

But there is another twist to the tale. You see, I had thought that, after the long hours and pressures of private practice, an academic post would be a stimulating but more relaxing option— teaching, giving the odd speech, doing more research, sharing my knowledge and experience with others keen to explore and navigate the world of financial law and generally giving back to a university which had, after all, changed my life. However, if anything, I am now working harder than ever!

The reason is P.R.I.M.E. Finance.[2] P.R.I.M.E. Finance stands for Panel of Recognized International Market Experts in Finance. There are, at the current time, 82 such experts who have been appointed and who, collectively, have more than 2,000 years of experience in the financial markets—judges, lawyers, central bankers, market practitioners, academics, and regulators from a diversity of jurisdictions and backgrounds around the world. P.R.I.M.E. Finance, which is based in The Hague, has been established both to help resolve and to assist judicial systems in the resolution of, disputes about derivatives and other complex financial transactions. Lord Woolf, the former Lord Chief Justice of England and Wales, chairs the P.R.I.M.E. Finance Advisory Board, and I chair the foundation's Management Board.

It is funny how things happen. Before retiring from Allen & Overy, while serving as chair of the ABA Section of International Law and just before the demise of Bear Stearns, the collapse of Lehman Brothers,

---

1.   It has been reported that Allen & Overy recently abolished this retirement age. Is this another positive reflection of the evolution to a more multicultural practice and recognition of the fact that the personal circumstances of the firm's lawyers around the world may be different? Or should I take it personally that the firm waited until I left to do this?!?

2.   *See* www.primefinancedisputes.org.

and the start of the 2008 financial crisis, I gave a speech in The Hague in which I questioned why it was that in so many jurisdictions there were special subject matter courts for everything from juvenile crime to tax and insolvency but not finance. And I pointed out how global trade and the World Trade Organization benefited from the WTO Tribunal, and also asked whether we needed an international body to support dispute resolution in the arena of global finance. Was global finance any less complicated or systemically relevant than world trade?

The speech was published as an article. Shortly after that the financial crisis was upon us, and financial crisis cases were fast arriving in domestic courts. A journalist at the *Financial Times* suggested that closer attention should be given to my article and the ideas in it. The Dutch authorities agreed to underwrite a gathering of experts from around the world to consider possible next steps. That roundtable discussion occurred immediately following a meeting of G-20 finance ministers in October 2010. By the following summer, The P.R.I.M.E. Finance Foundation had been created, and in January of 2012 it opened its doors for business. Within weeks it had its first case, and a few weeks after that, at the Global Arbitration Review awards ceremony in Stockholm, P.R.I.M.E. Finance received an award for "Best Newcomer." When you are in your 60s and somebody hands you a trophy for best *newcomer*—well, it doesn't get much better than that!

Our newspapers are full of articles about the debate regarding the role of regulation and regulators in mitigating systemic risk in the financial markets. By focusing instead on dispute settlement and judges, our project and the experts involved are following a different path. We did not think that it was wise to put all our eggs in the single basket of better regulation.

Another road less traveled to inspire us. Do you see how, in terms of career opportunities and job satisfaction, that can make all the difference?

So, exciting times. Many of you reading this book will be too young to have been, like me, a university student in the revolutionary 1960s. You missed that. Too bad. It was great. However, this may be about as exciting and revolutionary a time as the legal profession has known— especially if you are interested in a career in international law. But now let me share a few secrets about derivatives and how to pursue a career as a derivatives lawyer.

B. Why Derivatives Are Relevant

I remember being a terrible embarrassment to my daughter at a school event a number of years ago. She had a leading role in the student production of *Joseph and the Amazing Technicolor Dreamcoat.* My wife and I sat proudly in the front row. There is that bit in the plot when the Pharaoh is asking Joseph to explain the Pharaoh's dreams, and there is dialogue along the lines of "Seven fat cows, seven thin cows—Joseph, what does it mean? . . . Seven good years, seven bad years—Joseph, what can I do?" I shouted out from the front row: "Derivatives!" I can still remember my daughter, hands on hip, glaring back at me.

Well, like the good bard said, "All the world's a stage," and a few months later it was as if the theater lights were back on and I had been projected right into the plot of *Joseph.* In the Middle East, as part of a small delegation from the American Bar Association Section of International Law, I found myself in meetings in Damascus with Syria's Minister of Planning. He was lamenting the fact that Syria had just experienced a long period of drought, which could easily lead to famine. "Drought, famine, and I'm the Minister for Planning," he said. "But how can you plan for such things? How can you be expected to deal at the time with the extraordinary costs? What am I to do?"

This time I didn't shout. But slowly, my hand went up. "Have you heard of weather derivatives?" I asked when the Minister looked my way. "Put somewhat crudely," I explained, "your nightmare is the dream of some ice cream vendor or some air-conditioner manufacturer who can look to, but could not have counted on, record sales in what turns out to be a long, hot, and dry season. Still, next year's weather might be very different. Derivatives are a means of bringing your competing interests together, because each of you may be prepared to swap some of your upside in what would be a good year for the protection of a payout to help you cope with the risks of an unusually bad year."

C. What Are Derivatives?

A derivative is a contract that derives its value from something else. For example, like the weather derivative, the value of the contract might rise or fall depending on whether the temperature rises, or based on how many sunny days there are in a relevant period. Similarly, an option on a share of IBM or Apple is a contract that derives its value from, among other things, the price of an IBM or Apple share, as the case may be. Derivatives can be private, bilateral contracts (called over-the-counter or OTC transactions) or take the form of securities that are publicly traded on an exchange (i.e., listed options and futures).

D. Why Do You Do It?

Parties enter into derivatives contracts for a variety of reasons, but generally they are designed to manage or tailor a party's risk exposure. Derivatives can shift risks from where they naturally fall to where they can best be managed. For example:

- If you want to decrease your exposure (risk) to interest rate movements in relation to a loan portfolio that pays interest at a floating rate, you can enter into a swap with another party, where you make payments to the counterparty based on the floating-rate interest payments you receive on the loans, and the counterparty makes payments to you based on a fixed rate. In essence, this turns your floating-rate assets into fixed-rate assets and consequently reduces your risk to interest rate movements.
- If you want to increase your exposure or risk in respect of the S&P 500 or the Footsie 100 (because you think the index is going to rise), you can enter into options or swaps that make payments based on the level of the index.
- If you want to decrease your credit exposure or manage your risk resulting from bonds that you hold that were issued by a sovereign or corporate issuer, you can purchase credit protection by entering into a credit default swap that provides for payments when a credit event, such as a default by that issuer, is triggered.

I sit on the board of a company called MFX Solutions, Inc., which is an industry initiative designed to provide hedging protection for microfinance lending by using derivatives.[3] Microfinance loans are often very small, but they can be life-changing for the recipients.

---

3.   *See* www.mfxsolutions.com.

Muhammad Yunus demonstrated that the repayment record of such loans in developing economies, particularly where the loans were made to women or groups of them, could be at least as good as in the case of more conventional lending. But there was another risk lurking. Funding for microfinance was often provided in the first instance in hard currencies (dollars, euros), but the small loans needed to be in local currencies. However, when these local currencies depreciated against the hard currencies, that left a funding gap: even if the microcredit was repaid in full, there could be a shortfall in repaying the overarching hard-currency loan. Derivatives (e.g., currency swaps or options) can fill this gap. Derivatives (e.g., commodity swaps) can also help a single-commodity-dependent nation protect itself against what might be a crippling fall in the price of that commodity in the global commodity marketplace.

E. What Does It Involve?

Derivatives as a practice area sounds like it is a specialized or niche practice, but in many respects it is the last great generalist practice. A good derivatives lawyer will need to develop skills to deal with the following:

- Legal issues relating to contracts, secured credit, securities and commodities regulation, insolvency, conflicts of law, tax, banking, dispute resolution, and the list goes on;
- Structuring issues, like matching cash flows and allocating risks between the parties;
- Crisis management (ever heard of Nick Leeson at Barings, the collapse of Lehman Brothers, or a trader called the London Whale? Also see Asia in 1997, Russia in 1998, and Greece in 2012);
- Business development issues, like helping clients to establish new Web-based trading platforms; and
- Legislating and regulating for systemic risk, given the global nature of the business and its scale.

F.   When Does It Get Interesting?

Given the variety of the work, the sums involved (at last count, the OTC derivatives market alone measured US $650 trillion in notional amount trading), and the fast pace of the industry, it's always interesting. When something big happens, like the collapse of Lehman Brothers in 2008 and the financial crisis that followed, you get to be at the heart of some real headline-grabbing stuff.

G.   One Last Tip

As part of the financial markets law and regulation course that we teach at the LSE, I usually give an introductory lecture, "How to Succeed at a Derivatives Market Cocktail Party without Really Trying." I want our students to feel comfortable with the subject of derivatives as quickly as possible, and, of course, I want them to be a good advertisement for their LSE education (and their teacher!) when they talk about the course outside the classroom. Accordingly, in this first lecture, each student is given a small piece of paper, of a size that would fit into the palm of your hand, with five one-liners on it that can be dropped casually into conversations at a cocktail party. Each one-liner is designed to impress, and four of them vary from year to year. These reflect topical themes, so this year there might be one on credit derivatives or on collateral reform and efforts to harmonize the various jurisdictional laws on the taking of security, on clearing and the role of central counterparties, or on "flawed asset theory" and the recent split between the English and New York courts in the Lehman cases.

But the fifth one-liner never varies from year to year, and it is always just one word long: "Netting." I tell my students, just as I told the young lawyers at my firm, that if all else is forgotten, they should just remember: "Netting."

Whatever the question, they can always answer "Netting." (Why master agreements? Netting. Why special-purpose vehicles? Netting.) It will either be the right answer or, in any event, the person putting the question, knowing netting to be both so important and so complicated, will be too intimidated to second-guess the answer.[4] So, if you are in that all-important interview, seeking to be a derivatives lawyer, and you are at a loss for something that will impress . . . just remember "Netting"!

---

4.   "Netting" (and more particularly, "close-out netting") refers to a contractually agreed, and in some cases statutorily supported, basis for calculating or liquidating a single claim for settling or valuing the parties' broader derivatives-trading relationship. The parties may have entered into any number of derivatives trades over time, and at any particular time some of these trades may be "in-the-money" for one of the parties while other trades may be "out-of-the-money." Where the parties intend that their credit relationship should be viewed as "net," they will likely trade derivatives subject to the terms of standard form agreements that contemplate close-out netting when the trading relationship terminates. When that happens, the value of all outstanding trades is calculated, the pluses of the in-the-money trades are offset against the minuses of the out-of-the-money trades, and only the difference can be claimed. When one of the parties is bankrupt, netting prevents a trustee or liquidator from cherry-picking and making payments on transactions that are favorable and profitable for the insolvent party and refusing to make payments for transactions that are not profitable.

Netting is relevant for two closely related but somewhat different reasons: (1) *as an assessment of credit risk* (the enforceability of netting will determine the measure of exposure to a counterparty and the measure of the claim that can be asserted in subsequent court proceedings if the counterparty is insolvent), and (2) *as an assessment of capital costs* for regulated financial institutions. (The amount of capital that a bank must set aside as the cost of engaging in its derivatives business will turn on whether the bank's regulator recognizes the enforceability of its netting arrangements.) It has been estimated that netting can reduce a party's exposure to its counterparty by anywhere from 40 to 60 percent. With the notional amount of OTC derivatives trading in the system currently estimated to be on the order of US$650 trillion, that is potentially a lot of credit and systemic risk reduction!

What You Find Out After You Find Ice 4

by Bruce Horowitz

Many years later, as he faced the firing squad, Colonel Aureliano Buendía would remember that afternoon long ago when his father took him to discover ice for the first time.[1]

A. Finding Ice

Ice led me to a career in international law and to living in Ecuador. Not the magical ice at the beginning of *One Hundred Years of Solitude*, but rather a more mundane specimen found at motels everywhere in the United States in the summer of 1969—45 days and counting down to a concert that was about to lift off from Woodstock, New York. My particular career-defining piece of ice was waiting for me in a large, metal bin located under the outside staircase next to the parking lot at a motel in northern Alabama. I wasn't staying at that motel. We were traveling in a 1960 Plymouth with a nickname but no personality, driving across the country—away from what would

---

1. The first sentence in Gabriel García Márquez's *One Hundred Years of Solitude* (1967). In the original, "*Muchos años después, frente al pelotón de fusilamiento, el coronel Aureliano Buendía había de recordar aquella tarde remota en que su padre lo llevó a conocer el hielo.*"

be Woodstock, if the truth be told. We slept in a tent, not in motels. Motels were important to us that summer at the hot end of the 1960s, because motels in the South had swimming pools that seemed to be open to the car-driving public, and because all motels in the South had their ice machines outside under the stairs.

Yes, stolen motel ice was at the lip of the slope that drew me into a life of international law and a career in the tropics. And no, I was not caught cold-fingered by the Alabama State Troopers, nor have I been hiding out in the Andes ever since. Rather, a nameless stranger in front of me at that particular ice machine, while filling his own ice chest, saw our car's northern plates and asked where we were headed. "Out West," I said. "You?" "Peace Corps, Brazil," the stranger replied. And then he packed up his ice chest and headed east.

Back in 1960, when I was 11, I read an article written by a U.S. senator about his plan (were he to be elected) to train and send young people to foreign countries to work for peace and to help improve the lives of poor people. It was a thrilling concept. I was a young person, and this was for me. But young for the senator meant at least 18, and I was not that old yet. "Peace Corps, Brazil," the stranger had replied before he got into his car and drove east. Here I was now at 20, in the midst of reading George Orwell's *Homage to Catalonia*, wanting to be in any foreign country other than Vietnam, and wanting to help people.

By the time I got back to the Plymouth with that afternoon's stolen ice, and with a thunderstorm galloping toward us from the northwest, I had begun looking for a local library where I could spin a globe, close my eyes, and put my finger down on . . . Canada. Of course, at that time, if you wanted to serve in the Peace

Corps, you had to sit down rather than stand up beside the spinning globe—then you could close your eyes and put your finger down on . . . Ecuador.

A few weeks later, a human being bounced onto the surface of the Moon, under the light of which in the Grand Tetons I was mapping my future—and it was Ecuador. My senior year would no longer be dedicated to the English Country Aristocracy Honors History Project. Instead, that dedication would careen toward Ecuador Area Studies, the Economics of Development, the Politics of Underdevelopment, away from French and onto Spanish, Latin-American history, South American art, archaeology, and anthropology—and international law, for reasons beyond my control, as explained next.

B. Finding the Law

I was only 18 months old when I almost discovered a lawyer for the first time. I had somehow squeezed through the slats in our picket fence. When my mother could not find me in the backyard, she ran out the front door, and the first person she saw was our neighbor across the street sitting on his porch in his wicker rocker behind the pages of the afternoon newspaper. This neighbor was a lawyer and our town's own state legislative representative. After considering my mother's question as to whether he had seen her infant son anywhere, he folded back the top half of the newspaper, and pointed his pipe in the direction toward where he had seen me headed, given the time that had passed, and my forward momentum when he had first observed me waddling down the middle of Walker Street past his front porch.

The only other thing I knew about the lawyers in my town before I turned 16 was that one hunted squirrels and the other one lived with two Doberman Pinschers and hunted ducks. It was right after I turned 16 that I met the first lawyer whom I connected with the law, at the point when he was telling my family that we had nothing to worry about because my father had left the family's finances in good order. Thus was I introduced to the law.

This lawyer was clear-headed and a good person, and he spurred my interest in the law by taking down from his own library a well-read copy of Justice Holmes' *The Common Law* and placing it into my hands.

From then until law school, the only other lawyers I met on a professional basis were two draft counselors, who scared the crap out of me vis-à-vis the long arm and the mailed fist of the U.S. Selective Service System in reference to my low draft lottery number. It happened in my senior year, following directly upon my internationalist conversion by motel ice. So, in addition to learning about everything Hispanic-American that last year of college, I had taken up the self-guided (no-credit) study of the Selective Service (military draft) laws, where I suddenly fell or emerged into that tangential legal anti-universe dealing with the negative status and lack of rights of Stateless Persons.

Although this was but one small step into international law, it was like starting my legal career as the clam rather than the pearl diver. For someone who was just then traversing without a guide rope over page

95 of Jean-Paul Sartre's *Being and Nothingness*, "statelessness" was the perfect place to plant my flag on the mountain of international law.

C. Finding Peace

Three years have now passed. I am walking by myself through a swamp in the Ecuadorian Amazon Basin, wearing a red bandana and carrying a surveyor's transit, going into my fourth year as a volunteer surveyor in Ecuador. I have been lost in this section of Heaven for going on 10 hours now. The sun is sinking quickly, as it always does in a rainforest on the equator. I find a trail just after dusk, and when I get back to my village a few days later, there is a letter waiting from New York University (NYU) Law School. I had advised them that I would be staying in the Peace Corps another year and had asked them to hold my admission for just one more year. The letter from NYU advised me that it was to be now or never.

My time in the Peace Corps was an extraordinarily enriching part of my life, but it is almost all beyond the scope of an essay about why I got into international law. However, my experience there repeatedly told me that I could better serve as a lawyer, and after every new survey trek, my knees supported that conclusion. More important, an Ecuadorian friend of mine was about to become the first of his people to attend law school. Our plan was to work together after we had both graduated from law school.

Why had I chosen NYU? Because it was in the same city as the United Nations. During my three years at NYU Law School, I never set foot inside the United Nations or even checked to see what subway line to take to get to the UN Plaza. For some of us, the reasons why we start something have nothing to do with why we stay. I had chosen my college for a silly reason, but I stayed there because it (Brandeis University) was an amazing center of learning and social commitment. I chose Ecuador because it had mountains and was, I thought, small enough to learn all about in a senior year. I stayed there because it really was better than

Woodstock and a walk on the Moon combined, and because the people kept trying to teach me about wisdom, honesty, courage, beauty, and kindness.

I went to NYU Law School because of the UN, and stayed because NYU happened to be a factory that magically turned out handcrafted lawyers. I went to Alaska for a summer law clerkship and stayed for nine years because of the high quality and goodwill of the lawyers and judges, and because where else could a lawyer stand by his unwavering client over a hole in the ice a mile from land waiting for dinner to surface, and expecting any minute to turn into another chunk of ice himself. Twenty-two years ago, I returned to Ecuador for love. I have stayed in Ecuador for love, and because no one has ordered me to leave, yet.

During the Vietnam War, there was a slogan commonly used against the anti-war movement that went, "America, love it or leave it!" The U.S. Peace Corps later turned that phrase into a very successful recruiting campaign called "America, love it AND leave it."

D. Finding a Peaceful Place to Practice Law

Although it would surprise most U.S. citizens, many Latin-American immigrants migrate to places other than the United States. While most diplomats may have their hearts set on Paris, London, or Washington, D.C., lawyers who dream about living abroad, like other immigrants without a safety net, tend to be more open-minded, and find themselves traveling to and sometimes putting down roots in unlikely places.

I would venture a guess that most lawyers who move to other countries expect to return home within a few years. Their expectation is to learn things that will help them professionally upon their return home, and they may hope to make some money in the meantime. Most of them learn a lot, and some make some money during the learning process. A few of them become transnational practitioners. A few stay.

For some years now, the internationalization of the law and the cross-border harmonization of laws have been galloping to catch up with the globalization of the economy. Ignoring for the moment the issue of host-country lawyer backlash, it is becoming easier for foreign lawyers to work and stay, and sometimes even practice law. Of the 15 or so foreign lawyers I know who have stayed to live in Ecuador, about half of them (evenly divided between male and female lawyers) have married Ecuadorians, or have long-term relationships with Ecuadorians, or have long-term expectations for many short-term relationships with Ecuadorians. Only a few of the lawyers who do not arrive in-country through an embassy, a nongovernmental organization (NGO), or a transnational corporation find work as lawyers or as foreign legal consultants. Some of those who come down freelance get into the in-country legal field after starting out in administration, or as legal translators, or both.

In the United States, I worked for the Legal Services Corporation (or what the English used to call "the poor man's lawyer") in both litigation and law-office management, first in Alaska and then, for the last two years before I returned to Ecuador, back in my home state of Ohio. For the first four years after returning to Ecuador, I taught philosophy, logic, and economics and learned quite a bit about philosophy and logic; I also learned that being a good lawyer is easier—so much easier—than being a good teacher.

With another child on the way, I decided to return to the law, and while litigation was out for an unlicensed lawyer in Ecuador, I found a good firm that was interested in my management experience, combined with their hope that—as flatly translated from the Spanish legal phrase—I would be "intelligent in English." I had also come through the door with a decade's worth of useful practice in contracts, persuasive argument, negotiations, and some understanding of the U.S. legal system. I was found to be of some use, in a generalized way, when Ecuadorian clients of the firm needed initial guidance on a broad expanse of U.S. legal matters.

I became a good legal translator. I was introduced to intellectual property law at the local and international level with kind help from many local lawyers, to whom I shall be forever grateful. I also learned that one needs all five or six years of law school to prepare a simple, valid, civil-law power of attorney. Today, in addition to law office management, my practice involves international intellectual property, litigation risk and settlement analysis, international employment, agency and distributorship matters, and anti-corruption compliance and anti–public extortion work and training for individual clients and corporate client groups.

E. Meet the Bridge Ogre

Although I have been working with clients and training client groups since 1989 on how to get what they deserve from the government without submitting to an extortionist government functionary, it is only in the past three years that this work has become marketable as a specialty outside of the USA.

Some of the questions that I receive from "mentees" in the Mentoring program of the ABA International Section's Lawyers Abroad Committee have to do with whether it is possible to work in a country in the lower half of the Transparency International list without having to pay a bribe. And still serve your client. But what if . . .?

The answers are, in order: Yes. Usually, but in the end, you must always be ready to walk away (from the extortionist official, or sometimes from your client) rather than pay the bribe. The brief answer to "what if" questions is that you need to be creative; to never pay bribes, and to be known as someone who never pays bribes; to understand psychology, and to be able to apply to extortion situations that branch of psychology know as Negotiations; and to be willing to work very hard on extortion issues, just like you would on any other legal and practical issues.

F. Finding Your Own Path

Walking out of law school and into a foreign country where the people speak your language but have a different legal system will allow you to take a job as a legal messenger. Walking out of law school and into a foreign country where you speak their language will allow you to take a job as a translator. Walking into another country with a license to practice from back home, experience in at least one foreign language, and at least two or three years of experience in contracts, international trade, corporate law, accounting, American Depositary Receipts (ADRs), and negotiations will give you a boost when you go overseas to look for work with a foreign law firm. Having a similar background but in the areas of litigation, health law, human rights, environmental, employment law, and community development will give you a boost when you go overseas to work for a foreign or international NGO.

One interesting thing about living in a different legal culture is that one day you will truly understand that your legal system and their legal system have nothing in common; the next day you will truly understand that there is really no difference. Another interesting thing about all legal cultures is that each one has developed special overly long and ungrammatical incantations, which are fun to repeat, and which magically cause your nose to rise slightly and your lips to purse, and cause you to feel at least two centimeters taller.

On the other hand, unless you are Marcel Marceau, Charlie Chaplin, or Mario Moreno, the first thing you lose and the last thing you get back when you live in a new language is your sense of humor, even when you thought you never had one. It feels life-threatening when you are standing around in a circle with your newfound friends while one of them is telling a joke, and when the punch line comes, you have an out-of-body experience seeing everyone else laughing and looking at you while you display what is called a grimace. You begin to wish that jokes would never start, and if they start, would never end. Do not be discouraged; your sense of humor will return in five or six years, although during that time your misunderstood reactions to misunderstood punch lines will make you seem hypocritical, shallow, haughty, or distraught. Finally, the day will come when you can actually say something funny, intentionally funny. Then, after those five years of being laughed at, you will actually be laughed with, and at. You will have arrived. Humility and patience are good for a lawyer, as they are for anyone with some degree of power.

My Career as a Latin-American International Transactional Lawyer

5

by Andrew J. (Josh) Markus

A. Introduction

It's funny how perceptions change over time. I've written chapters on my career in every edition of *Careers in International Law*. Somehow I keep evolving. I am not even sure what this chapter will turn out to be as I am writing it, but it is my hope that it will be valuable to you if you are thinking about a career that involves international law or at least cross- border matters.

Even small companies are becoming globally aware. I am constantly being asked to help small and medium-sized companies go international or deal with selling their products or services outside of their home countries. In fact, even some much larger, household-name-type companies are struggling with what to do across borders. As new in-house counsel become a part of these large companies, they may have not dealt with many of the issues that confront business when it deals in other markets. So the situations I thought I would be faced with when I came to Miami, Florida, almost 36 years ago are now manifesting. Just like everything else in history, what has been happening could not have been anticipated those many years ago. Nevertheless, I feel certain that the next edition of this book will make this chapter seem outdated in ways I cannot anticipate. I am looking forward to meeting those challenges too with the skills I have developed and above all my ability to be adaptable as a lawyer and adviser to those who put their trust in me.

So, let me give you some insight into why I am an international transactional lawyer, what it is like to practice across borders and especially in Latin America, and what you can do to pursue a career in international law.

B. Why I Became an International Lawyer

I became a lawyer, naturally enough, because I had an early interest in the law. I remember reading a book, *So You Want to Be a Lawyer,* when I was in seventh grade. Whatever that book said to me, it must have been powerful, because here I am, all these years later, a practicing lawyer. To be fair, my father also helped me become the business lawyer I am today. He was a businessperson and exposed me to a wide variety of U.S. businesses. After that, I knew that the only kind of lawyer I wanted to be was a business lawyer.

So why did I then become an international business lawyer? Sometimes—and I think this happens more often than not—people find their special talents by accident. That was certainly what happened to me. My special talent is an ability to relate to things international. I became aware that I had a natural affinity toward the cultural aspects of international matters and that I related well to individuals from other cultures as a result of my travels in Europe in the summer of 1970. Travel was an eye-opening experience for me. I knew then that I was born to be international. I was going to law school. So I aimed to make myself an international lawyer. Little did I appreciate the long and interesting path I had chosen.

C. Law Firm Practice

How does talking about what it is like to practice in a law firm pertain to your path to international law practice? Well, let's assume that you are at the beginning, or nearly the beginning, of your career path as you read this chapter. As important as knowing that you want to do something international in the law is the environment from which you attempt to do it. This is important for several reasons:

- As a lawyer, you will be hired by a client for your legal skills. If you do not have top-of-the-line training, it is just that much harder to be a good lawyer. It will not serve you well to be a culturally aware lawyer if you cannot lawyer your way out of a paper bag.
- It is always easier to swim downstream. If you are fortunate enough to be hired and trained by a great law firm, you will have many more options in the future than if you start by hanging out your own shingle.
- If you practice law in an environment in which anything international is met with incomprehension, your international aspirations will wither and die unless you change to an environment that is supportive.

What big firms generally offer that small firms do not is the luxury of training and the opportunity to work on large transactions. You may not feel that this is a luxury at 11 P.M., while you work on reviewing due diligence or drafting an agreement for the client to review the next morning, but you will find, in hindsight, that you have learned much and, in fact, have an edge on most of your contemporaries. Large transactions bring into play all the skills that are required to do smaller transactions properly, but your firm can bill for these services and therefore has the luxury of allowing you to be on the team.

To be hired by a large, prestigious law firm in the United States, you must apply for and be accepted to do a summer clerkship at the firm. The lesson here is: plan early. Many a second- or third-year law student has approached me in January or later about becoming an associate in my firm. Invariably, they have been too late. With some foresight, that tardy law student could have been taking his or her place in the class of associates from which tomorrow's best international lawyers will come.

What small firms offer that big firms do not is hands-on experience at an early age. However seductive this may be, delay this gratification until you have received a good grounding in your chosen discipline. While there are exceptions, small firms often do not provide a viable platform for high-level international corporate work. On the other hand, small firms do provide a lawyer with the ability to handle a client's transaction from beginning to end and to be responsible for it. They also provide young lawyers with the opportunity (a mixed blessing, to be sure) to generate their own clients.

Medium-size firms (with 20 to 100 lawyers) seem to have the disadvantages of both large and small firms. The medium-size firm often does not provide hands-on experience early on or a viable platform for high-level international corporate work. It also does not provide a young lawyer with the opportunity to generate his or her own business. The trend appears to be toward larger firms, and even firms that would qualify in my numbering system as large (more than 100 to about 400 lawyers) are dissolving or being acquired at an accelerating rate. Thus, in the future it may be that there are two types of law firms—the mega firm and the small boutique firm.

D. What Does a Latin-American Transactional Lawyer Do?

My son used to ask me what I do all day. I used to be able to tell him. Now, I never know what will appear day to day. So sometimes I buy or sell a company or group of companies. Sometimes the companies are ultimately owned by a U.S. entity. Sometimes they are owned by non-U.S. entities, families, or individuals. Sometimes I help U.S. entities sell into Latin America. Sometimes I help Latin-American entities sell into the United States. Sometimes I draft and/or negotiate contracts, such as supply contracts, distribution contracts, or concessions of various types. Sometimes I represent Latin-American construction and infrastructure concession companies in bidding for large-scale U.S. public/private partnership projects. Sometimes I help Latin-American entities sell soccer broadcast rights to U.S. and non-U.S. television networks. Sometimes I help Europeans do business in the United States and U.S. companies do business in Europe. Sometimes I represent Latin-American or European or Asian individuals doing business in the United States. About the only thing I do not do is practice foreign (non-U.S.) law.

It used to be that lawyers had the luxury of doing one thing and variations of that one thing. No longer is that the case. I have always been a generalist—a lot broader than many lawyers are today. I've litigated. I've done real estate transactions and real estate finance. I've been a corporate lawyer, with all that that practice implies. I've been a public procurement lawyer. I've even been a construction lawyer. It's a good thing I have done all of this because if you are not flexible and adaptable, it is possible that you can find yourself pigeonholed in a practice that has withered or died.

The one constant in my practice is that just about every piece of business I do contains international aspects. I am a Florida Bar Board Certified Lawyer in International Law. The Florida Bar defines International Law as follows:

> International law is the practice of law dealing with issues, problems, or disputes arising from any and all aspects of the relations between or among states and international organizations as well as the relations between or among nationals of different countries. *Rules Regulating the Florida Bar 6–21.*

International practice can involve dealing with people or entities from another country, who are in the U.S. It can also involve dealing with people or entities from the U.S. who are in another country. The issues and problems can be in any industry, any discipline, and can be transactional or dispute-oriented. In other words, to be an international lawyer, one does not have to travel, speak languages, or even know anything about the laws of other countries.

However, to be a competent lawyer engaged in cross-border transactions, one must be competent in his or her home country's laws, be culturally sensitive, and be alert to the issues that arise when parties from different countries deal with one another. One must also realize that the laws of the other country demand that the U.S. lawyer consult non-U.S. counsel to understand the interplay. For instance, if I am engaged in an asset acquisition in which the assets are non-U.S. companies or operations, many issues arise under foreign law. The framework of my agreement, however, is U.S. (typically New York or Delaware) law. The entities involved are typically New York or Delaware corporations or other entities. Therefore, if some of the assets are in, say, a Brazilian *limitada,* questions as to title to the assets, rights attributable to the assets, and the like are certainly governed by Brazilian law. How do I know what the effect of these questions is on my transaction? Can I opine as to these aspects? No. Local counsel is an absolute necessity in this circumstance and plays a key role in the validity of such an acquisition.

E. How You Can Pursue a Career in International Law

My thoughts on this matter are strictly U.S.-oriented. I have practiced in large and small firms, in my own firm, in other people's self-made firms, and in old established firms. Whatever else firms have in common, for an international lawyer, the environment is the most important thing to consider. If the firm does not have a commitment to international practice, spend your time getting the best domestic law education you can and plan to move in a few years when you have a good, basic knowledge of what it is like to be a first-class lawyer.

Another aspect to consider on the path to "internationaldom" is that law firms are, at their essence, businesses. The exigencies of businesses often demand that their employees take paths different from those envisioned by them or the firm. This realization came to me one day when, having been hired to do international things in a law firm, I found myself doing real estate finance and development work instead. It was not what I was suited to do. It was not what I had planned to do. It was not even what my law firm had planned that I would do. But it was what needed to be done. I used the experience to make myself a more well-rounded lawyer, but I never forgot what I wanted to do with my career.

As it became apparent that my international opportunity was not going to occur in that firm, I did what is now commonplace—I changed firms. I did not move to a new firm for the money; my inducement was that the new opportunity would bring me closer to my career goal. That framework for viewing my career has led me to make several more changes in my career path. I practice now in Miami as chair of the International Practice Group of one of the largest and best-regarded Florida law firms doing corporate work, such as mergers and acquisitions, for Latin Americans and Europeans in the United States and for U.S. and non-U.S. companies in Latin America.

I have learned three important lessons:

1. *Be clear to yourself about what you want to do.* Try to understand your real career desires. You may find that you really don't want to be a lawyer at all, but a businessperson, an artist, or a writer. Or maybe (God forbid) you want to be a trial law-

yer. One thing is evident to me: If you aren't clear about what you really want to do with your career, you will find yourself moving in directions that you don't understand.

2. *Use what you learn, wherever and however you learn it, to further your chosen direction.* I could have been a real estate lawyer representing large institutions in complex real estate lending transactions or representing developers building large projects. Instead, early in my career, I took my good domestic law skills and applied them to representing non-U.S. investors and financiers of real estate projects. From there I developed relationships and gained experience in the transactional aspects of business representation. My clients started doing things other than real estate or introduced me to others who did things other than real estate. I factored all of these learning elements into my chosen direction and eventually began to do complex mergers and acquisitions domestically and internationally.

3. *Develop relationships early and often.* I have heard it said that the seeds for business one plants as a lawyer often take a long time to germinate. What is true is that your friends will be the ones who send you business and help you develop future contacts. We are in a relationship business. As a young lawyer, your friends will generally not be in a position to help you (or you, them) at the start. Be patient and keep contact with your friends. Make new friends along the way. Treat everyone with respect. Burn no bridges. Your friends are the key to your future.

Finally, do not despair if the job that you find initially does not appear to be international in scope. Just remember to keep focused on what you want to do as you go along and look for an opportunity to do it. Keep your eye on where you want to go and not where you are coming from. Assuming you still want to be an international lawyer, move in that direction. I do not think it is heresy anymore to suggest that you may need to move to several different firms before you feel that you are doing what you want to do. You might not make it on your first, second, or even third move, but keep your eye on what you want, and you will achieve it.

A Foreign (to the U.S.) Viewpoint on Practicing International Law

6

by Marcelo Bombau

A. Introduction

I have no doubt that U.S. attorneys and U.S.-trained attorneys are in the right place to practice international law. I state this because the world outside the United States generally looks to and follows U.S. trends, legal practice, and jurisprudence. Likewise, and in my opinion, of all the countries and economies of the world, the United States is the most international of all. Therefore, U.S. legal practice is not only the most competitive and highly regarded but also, by its nature or its adoption by foreign countries, the most international career of all.

While the concept of "globalization" takes business and clients all around the world (bringing their trusted attorneys with them), it is also true that many important jurisdictions (i.e., Brazil, India) have said "No" to any type of foreign professional activity in their jurisdiction. To this extent, doors are closing.

Although there are different ways of getting involved in international legal practice, together with the certainty that there are no road maps, it is equally true that many starting points do, in fact, exist. In this chapter, I will share my experience of how I got involved in international legal practice and give you my suggestions on how to approach said practice and best abide by its (unwritten) rules.

B. How It All Began

The majority of colleagues with whom I have spoken over the years agree with me in asserting that their involvement in international law did not occur overnight, and that many times they have had to change directions. My reality does not differ from theirs: I have had different experiences on my path to a full-fledged international practice.

I was probably influenced by my father and by the illusion that ambassadors lived a great life. I had always envisioned myself as part of the Argentine Foreign Affairs department. That is why I took all of the internationally related subjects at law school very seriously. However, one day, after speaking with another ambassador, I awoke from my dreamed lifestyle and suddenly found myself more interested in private international law rather than public international law.

I began my legal practice at an international, well-respected firm, where I have practiced for the last 30 years. This stability has been very helpful: the international atmosphere in this firm assisted my goal of becoming an international practitioner. Although my practice has evolved over the years in different directions—from being a labor law attorney to a commercial litigator—I have always tried to be as close to international legal issues as possible. In fact, I am now a mergers and acquisitions (M&A) attorney who is actively involved in an international practice. Quite often, practices are client-driven, and my experience is a confirmation of how client-driven needs change the course of one's personal history.

In my case, a U.S. multinational was in the process of acquiring a large company in Argentina, which was owned by a local businessperson. I had been hired to do the legal due diligence by the lead counsel of the U.S. multinational. After months of preliminary talks, the lead counsel presented the local businessperson with sizable drafts of stock purchases and shareholder's agreements in English. The local businessperson promptly asked where the Spanish versions were, to which the U.S. lead counsel conclusively stated that "95 percent of international deals are done in English." The local businessperson replied that his deal would then fall within the remaining 5 percent.

The next morning I received a call from the general counsel of the client, the U.S. multinational, who indicated that I would be leading all of the negotiations and drafting sessions going forward because otherwise the seller would simply walk away from the deal, having demanded—effective immediately—that the U.S. lead counsel be removed from the deal. This is how I got fully involved in all of the international aspects of an M&A transaction.

I continued to represent this client after the first deal closed, and in such capacity I have traveled throughout Latin America doing deals and trying to close the cultural gaps between Anglo and Latin ways of seeing things and doing business. Thus, the wrong answer given by the U.S. attorney and the subsequent regional legal needs of my client positioned me into the international arena. Because I did not want to suffer the fate of the U.S. attorney who had been removed from the deal, I started thinking of suggestions and tips for an international practitioner, which I would like to share. At least up until now, they have been very helpful to me and have been my guidelines in the international law arena.

C. Suggestions and Tips

In no specific order, here are several suggestions, which I recommend to any lawyer who wants to enter and stay involved in international legal practice:

1. *Choose a type of practice.* Be it private, in-house, or governmental, choose one that is coherent with your personal goals.
2. *Develop an expertise as much as possible.* Choose and specialize in a geographic region or a particular area of law, such as antitrust, tax, M&A, or environmental.
3. *Start as young as possible.* You might have to change courses more than once, but stay on your own path.
4. *Be the best lawyer you can be.* International attorneys are often both generalists and specialists, and their clients usually presume that they know almost everything.
5. *Join international organizations.* Contact U.S. embassies abroad and become active in associations such as the ABA Section of International Law, business communities, and Chambers of Commerce.

6. *Learn about different cultures.* Respectfully said, this is one of the most vital points, yet the most difficult to achieve for U.S. attorneys. Japanese, Argentine, U.S., and Swedish cultures, for example, differ enormously. You would be surprised to know how much I gained professionally with some U.S. clients simply by knowing how certain NFL teams had done on a given weekend!

7. *Find persons you are able to trust both personally and professionally; increase your international contacts.* A strong network of international contacts is one of the best assets an international lawyer can have. This will allow you to become known within your firm and by your clients as the go-to person. Always keep in mind that a client may expect a response in a very short time frame and does not always understand that you need to consult the laws of another jurisdiction. This is when your contact network is tested. Colleagues "on the same page" will help you win clients and be a truly 24/7 international lawyer. A good and reliable database takes years to build. Once you've built one, keep in touch with your contacts. By doing so, you will not only save time but also ensure that your clients get the best legal advice in a timely and reliable manner.

8. *Learn legal principles.* Countries around the world are ruled by very clear legal principles. Try to learn those broad principles.

9. *Learn the language.* Although this is not an absolute must, from my point of view, being able to speak more than one language, even with difficulties, will improve the rapport on both sides of the transaction.

10. *Keep up with the major events of the foreign country or region.* Presidential elections, economic booms, and thriving fields of business—I have come across many U.S. attorneys who have taken this point seriously and who have acquired an admirable knowledge of local events. Do the same.

11. *Make people feel that you are an equal.* Strange as an issue may seem, do not overreact or seem surprised when hearing the way legal business works in a different country. Show that you are trying to understand concepts that may differ substantially from U.S. practices.

12. *Write articles in international publications.* Do not rule out jointly authoring articles with foreign lawyers.

13. *There is no need to restrict yourself to legal advice.* Many clients—especially those in the international field—do not want involvement in the "nuts and bolts" of the legal issues. Although interested in the basic legal concepts that you will be negotiating, they will welcome some "business talk" and advice.

14. *Always rely on "common sense."* Western culture is based not only on the law but also, in all aspects of life, on common sense. Apply common sense to every new matter and do not stop until you have all of your questions answered. An international lawyer is required to be extremely focused on all of the details irrespective of jurisdiction. The deal determines the territorial scope of your practice, with the support of colleagues in the jurisidictions affected. But pay attention to common-sense details: being lazy on the details and not understanding the whole picture may compromise your advice.

15. *Avoid prejudice.* Human beings—which species includes international lawyers—sometimes bring a fair amount of prejudice to the table. Do not compare what you know from your legal system, or how well or badly it works, or, even worse, what should or should not be in any given deal. Focus, for your own sake and, most important, for your client's sake, on fully comprehending the ground rules and adapting to them.

16. *Non-written rules.* An international lawyer will understand—mainly in emerging markets—that certain rules are not formal but political. You need to protect your client not to put the system on trial.

17. *Availability.* A main "mark" for international lawyers is availability. Time zones sometimes render contact difficult. Use technology for your own benefit. Do not become "workaholic," but you should find ways to benefit from technology to become a "high-tech" lawyer, thereby making yourself available for quick communication. International clients feel safe when they know you are easily reached. If you notice that scheduling an international call with you takes more than a reasonable amount of time, be prepared for bad news. Difficult communication now can be attributed only to you; you can no longer

blame the fax machine or the availability of international telephone lines.

Of course, being an international lawyer is demanding and can be difficult at times, but no other area of law practice will give you opportunities to meet interesting people, interact with different cultures and languages, and expand your knowledge of the law beyond unimaginable limits.

The road to becoming an international attorney may seem endless and unclear, but, at least in my case, the path in and of itself is truly rewarding.

Part 2
Private Sector

A Solo Practitioner's Pathway to International Law Practice

7

by Aaron Schildhaus

People have asked how someone born in a small town in Vermont, who had never traveled outside North America, would have a passion for international law. Either I was born too soon or international law became popular too late. I was passionately interested in the concept but frustrated by the reality. For example, when I went to law school, I took a one-semester elective titled International and Comparative Law. It was the *only* course on international law that was offered. Today, the Washington College of Law, American University, prides itself on having one of the richest curricula in the field of international law. It now lists more than 100 courses on international law and offers J.D. and LL.M. degrees in six countries outside the United States.

How did I, a solo practitioner, end up in the field of international law?

When Lyndon Johnson was President, he advised Americans to see their own country first before venturing abroad. After taking his advice and seeing quite a few states, I still felt there must be something of interest outside the United States, so in the summer before my last year of law school, I ventured outside North America for the first time. All summer long, I traveled around Europe.

It was an eye-opener, and I haven't closed my eyes or ears since. I was determined to be an international lawyer, whatever that meant.

The following spring, my law school published a "Placement Publication," which had all of the graduating seniors' pictures with categories of information filled in by each of us. Among the categories was "Type of Practice Sought." I listed "International Law (Commercial Aspects)." Another category was "Location Preferred." My entry: "Abroad." In the late sixties, such aspirations were as foreign to most Americans as were other countries. I remember the jibes—people pointing at me and laughing: "International Law . . . Abroad . . . ha, ha, ha." In fact, I am still having the "last laugh." I have been practicing international law now for more than 40 years.

A.   Entering the Field of International Law

Finding a job in international law was a major challenge in the early 1970s, given that so few professionals recognized it as a separate practice area. My first job after graduation was with a law firm in Washington, D.C., where I was assigned to help draft and codify municipal legislation that could be standardized for computer applications; those were the very, very early days of computer use by lawyers. After I passed the D.C. Bar, I found employment in Boston as a staff attorney in the legal department of an insurance company with home offices in the United Kingdom. Other than the fact that I occasionally met a chap with a British accent, there was not too much international law there, either.

Like many others now in the field, my first jobs were not international. But I was determined to put my legal training to work in a productive way that would expose me to a broader world—one that would not end at the shores of the Atlantic or Pacific oceans. In my mind, the practice of international law was something that could not be done effectively unless one had the chance to live and experience different legal systems, different cultures, and different languages. Thus, as I honed my basic legal skills with increasing frustration at the lack of any international connection, I took whatever money I had and traveled across the Atlantic. However, U.S. employers could not understand anyone not working 50 weeks a year and untold hours per week. Travel was expensive, time was short, and jobs were on the line. Wherever I worked, I kept seeking the international exposure and the right angle to get me into the field.

Luck always plays its part. It is often said that if you try hard enough and long enough, you can create your own luck. It is probably more accurate to state that if you look around intelligently and put yourself in the right places, chance may bring an opportunity to your door. The difficulty lies in spotting the opportunity and persevering to turn that chance into a lucky break. My chance came when I was hired as an in-house lawyer by PepsiCo, Inc. in its leasing and financing division. Thanks to the mentoring of my immediate boss, I learned the nuts and bolts of drafting complex financial and corporate transactions, the niceties of understanding abstruse provisions of contracts, and the process of properly shepherding closing documentation. This experience enabled me to appreciate the wordsmithery we lawyers do, despite its often pejorative connotation.

I learned to be precise, because the discipline of precision enables one to cut through linguistic and cultural differences in order to express oneself accurately and be clearly understood by others. Later, when learning and working in foreign languages, this skill became paramount in my arsenal of legal tools. It remains so to this day, and I am still grateful to my boss and mentor for insisting on the highest standards in transaction analysis and drafting that I was able to put into practice to complete the deals.

Although I handled a few deals involving offshore issues and parties, I was hungry for more international work, and PepsiCo. proved to be a major stepping-stone to my career: It had an excellent law department and a terrific and supportive general counsel. When I expressed my interest in going to Europe, I was not discouraged. To the contrary, the company reimbursed me for the cost of my first French language lessons. And so, with the blessing of my general counsel, I was granted a sabbatical, which has been in place since 1975.

B. My Move Abroad

I decided to move to Paris, where I was certain I would be greeted with open arms many job offers. My theory about moving to Paris then was simple: If a firm did not have to pay my moving costs and cost of living, it would—so I assumed and hoped—jump at the chance to employ me as a "local hire."

I arrived in Paris in the summer of 1975, the time of year when Parisians think of summer holiday, not summer hiring. However, in September Paris was transformed into a beehive of activity. Shortly thereafter, I landed a job with a Franco-German law firm that was a spin-off of the largest French firm at the time. It was a bit of a fluke, because the senior partner of the firm wanted a native-speaking American lawyer who could speak German and lived in Paris. Although it was perfect for me, it soon became obvious that neither my German nor my French were at the necessary levels. I rose to the challenge, steadily improved my German and my French, and began to cope with all of the challenges of integrating myself into a new and very different culture. I was assigned almost immediately to work on a global acquisition project for a major Canadian multinational.

After about a year, my youth, my optimism, and the excitement of Paris propelled me to leave the security of the law firm and strike out on my own. Unfortunately, I did this much too soon, as I was too young and inexperienced and, consequently, seriously unprepared for such a venture.

However, despite the hard times, there were many kind, helping hands along the way. An American lawyer, in-house general counsel with a major international oil company, gave me corporate work and became a good friend; a German lawyer gave me legal consultation work involving U.S. law and became a lifelong friend; a Paris law firm with a conflict referred to me a fascinating U.S. litigation case with multi-country parties, requiring me to conduct discovery in France; and an American lawyer with a major Wall Street firm's Paris office let me use the office to receive clients. Many others, mostly Parisians, went out of their way to help me.

Surviving as a solo practitioner in Paris is not one of the easiest things to do, and I would not recommend it for the faint of heart. Not that I was particularly strong-hearted; I just did not know any better. Nevertheless, through targeted networking I managed to get some major, but mostly minor, European companies as clients for outbound business to the United States. Unfortunately, without an American law firm supporting my efforts, the clients all ended up, quite naturally, with the American law firms that were handling their business in the United States. This was a good example of lawyering one's way out of business.

C. Returning to the United States and Joining the Section of International Law

In 1986, I returned to Washington, D.C., with no idea where to begin, as I had lost most of my prior contacts. Nevertheless, I had decided that I had the right skills to be a great international lawyer, and I was determined to succeed in international law from a base in the United States. I was not interested in any other kind of law. I figured, at that stage in my life, that if I were to take a job dealing solely with domestic legal issues, I would never be able to get off that treadmill. How does a now-middle-aged solo practitioner without business compete as an international lawyer in the international capital of the world? How could I get business, and how could I meet the right people with whom to network?

A lawyer I met in the process of knocking on doors in Washington, D.C., told me that the best way to network was to get active in the right organization. I will never forget this advice. Within months of returning to the United States, I attended an ABA annual meeting in New York City. As a business lawyer, I attended both the Business Law Section and the International Law Section programs. Very quickly, I found my new home in the International Section. The focus was global, and the members were open and friendly. Most of them shared my international interests, different language capabilities, and living experiences abroad. I joined committees, began attending meetings, and became active in the Section. It is the single most important and effective organization for practicing international lawyers in the world, and being a part of it is rewarding every day. I never looked back.

D. My Most Gratifying Professional Experiences

Fairly quickly after joining the ABA and becoming active in the International Section, I decided to set up my own law firm, The International Business Law Firm. Joining the ABA and setting up my own international law firm are among the most gratifying things I have done. Although I eventually left the law firm I founded, I never left the Section. The more involved I became in it, the more I honed my skills as an international lawyer, due in no small part to the Section's resources.

Through its committees and members, the Section is an outstanding and accessible reservoir of exceptional legal talent.

Since joining the International Section, I have dutifully attended the Council meetings, where the major international issues are discussed and debated. Now I am a member of the Council and am honored to sit at the same table with so many accomplished and expert international lawyers. I still attend as many substantive programs at meetings as possible, which allows me to remain on the cutting edge of international legal issues and developments and to gain the perspectives of the experts who participate in the panels and on the scores of committees in the Section.

In addition, the Section's activities outside the United States, whether International Legal Exchange (ILEX) trips, international bar leader trips, or fall meetings in Brussels, London, or elsewhere, always bring a special dimension to Section membership. As an inveterate traveler, I participate in these trips whenever I can, and I never regret a moment of them. They combine so much that is positive in international law practice: interesting places, interesting people, current and pertinent information about major international legal issues, and most of all, a sense of continually contributing to global understanding and good relations among members of the legal profession around the world.

Through Section activities, I have become conversant in an amazing variety of international legal issues, and I have had the opportunity to meet lawyers from every branch of the profession: law professors, U.S. and other government lawyers, those working for international and multilateral organizations, in-house corporate counsels, other solo practitioners like myself, law students, and the young and the old, hailing from Africa, Latin America, Eastern and Western Europe, Asia, and the Middle East.

I have been exposed to the great legal minds of our generation: Justice Stephen Breyer, Judge Thomas Buergenthal, Harold Burman, Hans Corell, President Valery Giscard d'Estaing, Marsha Echols, Dean Claudio Grossman, John Jackson, Henry King, Dean Harold Koh, Boris Kozolchyk, Monroe Leigh, Eleanor Roberts Lewis, Ramon Mullerat, Betty Southard Murphy, Justice Sandra Day O'Connor, Peter Pfund, Ibrahim Shihata, Louis Sohn, David Stewart, K. K. Venugopal, Don Wallace, Ruth Wedgwood, and many, many others. Not only have I had the opportunity to meet these giants of the profession and been able to share their thoughts and ideas, but I have also worked with several and am honored to have many of them as friends. I am very grateful to my colleagues and proud of them and their achievements.

One of the great occasions of my career was also my biggest surprise: when I received the Mayre Rasmussen Award in recognition of my contributions to the advancement of women in international law. As the only male recipient of the award to date, I found myself in extraordinary company: Mayre Rasmussen, Lucinda Low, Dianna Kempe, and Rona Mears. I could accept the award only with the understanding that we have but scratched the surface. Deborah Enix-Ross, the first African-American chair of the Section and a subsequent recipient of the Mayre Rasmussen Award, appointed a Diversity Task Force, on which I was proud to serve. I am honored to have served as chair of the first Section in the ABA with a diversity officer, responsible for promoting and ensuring continued and increased tolerance of differences in race, gender, national origin, age, abilities, sexual preferences, and other types of diversity in the Section.

Several other events were unforgettable for me and occurred in 2008-2009, when I chaired the Section: leading a historic ILEX delegation to India and forming the India Committee; being made an honorary life member of AIJA (Association Internationale des Jeunes Avocats), and most of all, being inducted as a Nigerian Chief in a ceremony that took place in Washington, D.C., at our 2009 Spring Meeting. I am proud of my title, "OloyeBaamofinGbogbogbo of Owoland," and I am proud of the many great and wonderful Nigerian lawyers who are now members of the Section.

E. Conclusion

My career in international law started many years ago, and it continues to evolve. I am now living in Buenos Aires and studying Spanish, while continuing my practice focus on anticorruption law and corporate international practice. Every day brings exciting challenges, more knowledge, and new friends. I am helping to make a difference in the world by working on important policy matters in committees, on the Council, and with the larger ABA, and by my continued interaction with the global profession of law. I look forward to each day with the same eagerness I did 40 years ago.

Fair Winds and Following Seas: A Career in Admiralty Practice

8

by Michael Marks Cohen

A. Introduction

Admiralty is the granddaddy of all international commercial law, with antecedents that stretch back to Biblical times. For more than 500 years, written maritime codes have covered carriage of goods by sea, general average, salvage, marine insurance, seamen's rights, and arbitration. In the absence of statutes, judge-made rules have been applied to collision, shipboard personal injury, carriage of passengers, shipbuilding, ship finance, and ship chartering. In modern times, these traditional subjects have been supplemented by shipping regulation and water pollution controls. Although now there are many treaties and much local legislation, the courts continue to play a very active role in shaping the law to changing circumstances.

Like 60 to 70 percent of my generation, I was drawn to the admiralty bar by seagoing experiences, having served for three years as a naval officer on a destroyer between college and law school at Columbia. At the time, many individuals opted for naval or Coast Guard service rather than be drafted into the Army during the period between the Korean and Vietnam wars. One consideration was to parlay our legal training and military experience into a career so we could put our time in the service to good use.

After clerking for Stanley H. Fuld, the chief judge of the New York Court of Appeals, I started out in maritime practice as a trial lawyer with the Admiralty & Shipping Section of the U.S. Department of Justice in Washington, D.C. Three years later I joined an admiralty law firm in Manhattan, and I have been in private practice ever since. Currently I am of counsel to Nicoletti Hornig and Sweeney.

Admiralty principles and concepts are generally similar throughout the world. In many respects, maritime law is a sort of written and unwritten uniform commercial code that has been adopted by each country with local variations. Foreign precedents—especially those from England and other common-law jurisdictions like Canada, Australia, New Zealand, Hong Kong, Singapore, and South Africa—are frequently cited and are highly regarded.

There is a good deal of maritime litigation in the United States, mostly in the federal courts, as federal law is controlling. Generally, apart from personal injury cases, there are no jury trials.

Maritime law strives for uniformity. Therefore, new developments are followed not just locally but nationally and internationally. Moreover, it is the only area of federal law where older cases are commonly more highly regarded than more recent ones, partly because maritime matters formed such a substantial part of the work of the Supreme Court up until just after World War I. A remarkable number of current procedures in federal civil litigation, which are intended to promote fairness and simplicity, have their origin in admiralty practice—some of it more than 150 years old and/or of foreign derivation. Routinely, many disputes are not taken to court at all but instead are voluntarily submitted to arbitration in London or New York, often before commercial arbitrators rather than lawyers.

B. Disadvantages

There are a few disadvantages in admiralty practice. Most cases involve claims of less than $250,000; few go as high as $10 million. Such blockbusters as the *Titanic, Andrea Doria, Amoco Cadiz,* and *Exxon Valdez* come along only once every decade or so. Hardly ever is there a case that will make or break the client. Although world events have an immediate impact on day-to-day practice, in reality, shipping involves the legs rather than the heart of world trade.

Compensation is adequate but not fabulous. Much of the work comes from a comparatively small number of marine insurance companies, a situation that fosters price competition. In addition, the nature of the work makes it difficult to leverage—that is, to put more than one associate on a case with a partner. These factors force admiralty lawyer income levels below those of colleagues in other fields.

Shipping is not an explosively expanding field. Moreover, it is susceptible to large cyclical swings. Very few new domestic shipping companies are formed. Established companies do not change legal advisers very often. Most new clients are referrals from existing clients, or from local corporate law firms, or from out-of-state or foreign admiralty lawyers.

C. Advantages

For all of the disadvantages cited, there are quite a number of advantages to the practice. Because of the historical role of London in marine insurance, salvage, ship finance, and ship chartering, all admiralty lawyers and their clients throughout the world speak English. It is not necessary to be fluent in a foreign language to have a successful practice and a rewarding career.

The bar is small—almost a craft guild—with only a few thousand full-time practitioners here and abroad. Frequent contacts among the lawyers are maintained across state lines and international boundaries. Locally, in the cities where they practice, admiralty lawyers have a well-deserved reputation for professionalism and courtesy in their relations with one another.

There are several unusually active national and international bar associations. The number of maritime lawyers practicing together in a firm is usually small. In New York, a number of the maritime firms concentrate on shipping law, with perhaps some additional work in aviation and the sale of bulk commodities that are shipped by sea, such as oil, grain, and iron ore. A few New York firms, and one or two others elsewhere in the country, may have as many as two dozen admiralty partners and associates, but for the most part, there are usually fewer than 10 maritime lawyers in any given firm. Increasingly, those lawyers can be found as a small department of a large corporate law firm.

There are frequent opportunities for travel to interesting places— most often London, Tokyo, and Hong Kong. Clients tend to be very practical, often colorful figures. The risks in shipping appeal to individuals who enjoy gambling for high gains in a short period. The sums can be large. Time differences, geographic separation, weather uncertainties, human errors, and the need for quick decisions call for analytical skills and imaginative tactics that are not usually found in a non-maritime commercial practice.

It is definitely not a stuffy field. Practice is very closely tied to the headlines in the newspapers.

Natural disasters such as earthquakes and hurricanes, as well as predictable seasonal events, such as ice in the Great Lakes, promptly cause clients to seek advice. The same is true for world events—wars in Iraq and Afghanistan, pirates off Somalia, refugees fleeing in small boats at sea, the decline of the dollar, turmoil in the Middle East. When combined with individual calamities—groundings, oil pollution, engine breakdown, pilfered liquor, rotting fruit, leaking holds—the work can be very stimulating. It is not only intellectually challenging but fast-moving: lawyers are commonly called for spot advice while a crisis is in progress.

The overall lifestyle in maritime practice is generally much more relaxed than in large corporate work. Time can usually be found for bar association efforts, teaching, writing for professional journals, and, most important, being with family. Practicing admiralty law ought not to destroy your marriage or ruin your children. In recent years, a very high percentage of associates joining admiralty firms have been women. There is widespread religious diversity at the bar. Greater racial diversity would be welcome.

D. Training

Although not essential, an admiralty course in law school would be helpful, not only for careers in practice but also for those seeking clerkships with federal judges in port cities. Experience at sea with the Navy, Coast Guard, or Merchant Marine is useful but, again, not a prerequisite. Perhaps the best training for admiralty practice is to write an article on a maritime law subject for a student journal in law school.

E. Starting Out

A good place to start out is the Torts Branch of the Civil Division of the U.S. Department of Justice. Nearly all admiralty cases involving the federal government are handled centrally by about a dozen admiralty lawyers in Washington, D.C. and San Francisco. There are a few openings annually.

In private practice, New York is by far the biggest market. There are new jobs for perhaps two dozen associates with maritime firms there each year. Outside New York, all of the major seaports, the Great Lakes, and the inland rivers combined may produce an equal number of openings. Firms can be difficult to locate just through *Martindale-Hubbell*, but many of the leading firms are identified in the *Chambers USA Guide* and *The Best Lawyers in America*. All firms that have at least one lawyer who is a member of the Maritime Law Association of the United States are listed at the website, www.mlaus.org.

The China Bug | 9

by Michael E. Burke

A. Introduction

I'm very proud to be from New Jersey (as you could tell
from the onsite guide to the Section's 2012 Spring Meeting). When I was growing up, my father always said:
"What New Jersey makes, the world takes." He was right.
New Jersey is a very international place. On my block,
we had first-generation immigrant families from Ireland,
India, and other places, as well as many second-genera-
tion immigrant families. New York, perhaps the most international of cities, was 25 miles away. Growing up in
New Jersey means understanding that we are part of a
larger, global community.

Being from New Jersey also means living by a certain
work ethic. My first job was working for my uncle's landscaping company. Landscaping in the New Jersey summer heat is tough. My uncle was the most demanding boss
I have ever had; he expected me to be at work at 7 a.m.
every day, work hard, and do things right the first time.
Living up to that ethic—taking pride in what you do, and
doing your job to the best of your ability every day (even
on the days where you'd rather be doing something else)—
is an important step in becoming an international lawyer.

Good lawyers—especially those with an international focus—need to invest the time and effort to build their skills and provide the best service to clients every day.

B. Getting Educated

I never had a "Eureka!" moment about becoming a lawyer. There were plenty of lawyers in my hometown, but I don't remember being inspired by any of them to practice law. Nobody in my immediate family—my parents, aunts and uncles—was a lawyer. My real childhood dream was to occupy right field for the Boston Red Sox, but my lack of athletic ability prevented that.

Although I didn't specifically think about becoming a lawyer, I was very interested in international relations and history. I always participated in the model United Nations program. I even took a college course at Boston College (during the summer between my junior and senior high school years) on Soviet foreign policy, and then convinced one of my high school history teachers that I should spend part of my senior year doing an independent study project on Soviet history (yes, there was a Soviet Union back then). Further, I was very fortunate that my parents took me—and sometimes sent me—overseas to learn about different countries and cultures. The international bug bit me before the lawyer bug.

I attended the University of Michigan for my freshman year of college, and that's where the international bug began to change into a China bug. Kenneth Lieberthal was the professor in the Comparative Politics class I took during my freshman year, the same time Professor Lieberthal was writing his seminal work *Governing China: From Revolution Through Reform*. That class was the first time I remember thinking that China was a place about which I wanted to learn much more.

After my freshman year, I transferred to Georgetown University's School of Foreign Service (SFS). The SFS has perhaps the most challenging, most internationally focused curriculum of any college program in the United States. I'm fortunate to have been able to complete that program, and it was the perfect fit for my interest in international affairs. While at SFS, I studied abroad at the Catholic University of Antwerp in Belgium, passed my foreign language proficiency exam in French, was selected for the school's Scholars Program, and wrote two theses, one on conflict resolution in Northern Ireland and one on defense and security integration within the European Union.

Successful international lawyers know more than one language, and college is one of the best places to become multilingual. Also, good international lawyers appreciate and can operate in other cultures and contexts. College is one of the best places to become exposed to other cultures, such as through club activities or study abroad programs. If you didn't learn a foreign language in college or study abroad, there are opportunities to do so after college and even during (or after) law school.

After college, I worked for Exxon Research and Engineering in New Jersey, developing cost models and estimates for overseas refinery projects. I also worked for U.S. Senator Dianne Feinstein as a staff assistant, opening and responding to constituent letters and requests that touched on foreign affairs issues. After the close 1994 congressional mid-term election, I realized that I needed some sort of advanced degree, and my strong preference was to enter law school.

C.   Law School: What, When, and How?

Attendees at the Section of International Law's *Pathways* programs, which feature experienced international lawyers offering guidance to law students and young lawyers on developing an international practice, have specific questions about how to direct their law school experience.

Prospective and current law students ask whether they should go to, or transfer to, a specific law school in order to become an international lawyer. I believe that students should attend the law school where they feel the most comfortable and believe they have the best chance at completing a comprehensive legal education. Prospective students should not worry about whether a certain school has a robust international curriculum, as most law schools now have some form of international law curriculum. There are also many international law summer programs that may supplement a school's existing curriculum.

At *Pathways* programs, I am also often asked whether there are any specific classes one should take in law school. Prospective international lawyers should take their school's introduction to international law course, which generally focuses on public international law, and should take (if available) a course on international economic relations. But there is no strict blueprint for law school classes that will create an international lawyer, as many of the essential skills for an international lawyer (e.g., language and cross-cultural appreciation) may not be offered as part of a law school curriculum.

I graduated from Georgetown University Law Center (GULC) in 1998. I was fortunate that GULC has a robust international curriculum, but I chose GULC because it was in Washington, was a comfortable place, and offered a great legal education. GULC's international law curriculum was a bonus, but wasn't necessarily one of the primary factors in my decision to attend. Put another way, you should attend the program in which you think you have the best chance to excel.

At GULC, I took the introduction to international law course, the international trade and investment course, and courses on European Union and Korean law, respectively. I also took courses on venture capital transactions, alternative dispute resolution, corporate taxation, and trusts and estates. I served on the staff of, and as an editor for, the journal *The Tax Lawyer.* One should seek a well-rounded legal education—take courses from a wide range of areas, including (but not limited to) international law. Participate in a journal, even if it does not focus on international law. The point of law school is to produce well-rounded lawyers who are versed in several areas of the law and who can think, analyze, communicate, and write effectively.

If your school doesn't have a specific course you're looking for, consider an independent study/directed research project. I would be remiss if I did not mention one of my law school professors and the tremendously positive impact he has had on my career. Jim Feinerman is one of the best-known and best-qualified China experts in the United States. He is also one of the best, most generous people you will ever meet. Professor Feinerman was the professor for my corporations class, and he spent a fair amount of time in that class discussing how corporations were regulated in Japan and China. The comparative analysis struck a chord with me; the China bug that was planted in Professor Lieberthal's class had begun to find an outlet.

During my second year, GULC did not offer a course each semester on Chinese law (it does now), and I asked Professor Feinerman how I could learn more about the development of the Chinese legal system. The results of these discussions were two supervised research/

independent study projects during my second and third years of law school that, in turn, resulted in my first two law review articles. I suggest that you develop a good relationship with your professors, especially international law professors, and learn from their experience. I am still in contact with Professor Feinerman, and he remains a tremendous resource for me as I continue to develop my career. A professor's value to law students is not limited to the classroom. If your school permits it, think about undertaking a directed study/independent research course; if your school's curriculum seems to be missing a course, don't be afraid to develop one.

D. Getting a First Job: How, Where, and Why?

At *Pathways* events, participants often ask if, in an interview process, they should indicate an interest in a specific practice area to increase their chances of being assigned international work. It's appropriate to express an interest in an area of the law if your interest is genuine, but don't express an interest in an area just because you think it is a way to get international work. One of my classmates told interviewers that he wanted to do project finance work. He wasn't really interested in that work, but he thought it was a good way to get international work. He was hired into a project finance group at a large D.C. firm, and he did project finance work for projects in Los Angeles, Phoenix, and Milwaukee. He got frustrated at the lack of international work and left the firm after 18 months.

One other note: when approaching a potential interview, you should research the firm and the interviewer so you can understand what the firm does and does not do in terms of international work. An interviewee once told me that she thought my former firm's Korea practice was of interest. At the time, that firm didn't have a Korea practice, and her statement was a factor in not inviting her back for a second-round interview.

I am also often asked whether a person who is interested in international law should join a large law firm in New York upon graduation. The practice of international law isn't confined to large law firms or even to firms in New York. Sophisticated and interesting international legal work can be found in many cities. In determining where to go after graduation, you should consider a place where you can develop your career and can get immediate access to interesting and rewarding work. Also, you might want to think about living in a place where you can have a decent quality of life.

After graduation, I joined a large law firm based in Seattle—quite a change for someone born and raised in New Jersey and educated in Washington, D.C. I went west to be a part of the dot-com explosion, with the expectation that a lot of interesting international work would flow from emerging technology companies. I chose to go to Seattle, and not a firm in New York, because I wanted to get a lot of client service responsibility as quickly as possible, be able to build an expertise, and be at a place where I thought I could spend the majority of my career.

E. Becoming a Good International Lawyer

When I met my mentor partner on my first day at my first job, he told me, "I always thought international law was a waste of time." Nonetheless, I learned much from my mentor partner. He taught me how to closely read a contract and identify potential problem areas. I knew that he expected me to know how an agreement worked, in addition to putting the right words on the page. I knew that he expected that the maximum amount be communicated in the minimum number of words. He hated even the hint of sloppiness in drafting.

He also taught me the importance of managing expectations and how to communicate effectively with clients within and outside the firm. He was a good mentor and he taught me how to be a good lawyer, because in order to be a good *international* lawyer, you need to be a good lawyer first. That's more than a tautology. The skills needed to become a good lawyer, such as being a good communicator, well organized, a good writer, and a good issue spotter, are doubly important for a good international lawyer. It shouldn't matter if you're building those skills doing non-international work. You need to do all you can as a young lawyer to build basic practice skills—the building blocks for a long career. Take the time to perfect those skills, because it is a worthwhile investment.

I started doing international work by networking with the firm's other lawyers, including the chair of that firm's international practice; understanding who had international work; and offering to help with whatever tasks needed attention. In most cases, having a mentor partner does not preclude you from working for other lawyers in your firm. Don't be shy about volunteering to help out with projects that interest you. Also, be persistent; you may not get on the first project for which you volunteer, but after a while you'll find yourself in a core group of go-to lawyers.

To become a good international lawyer, you may have to take a risk and step outside traditional legal practice. Some of the most interesting international work is performed at government agencies (like the Office of the U.S. Trade Representative and the State Department), nongovernment organizations, think tanks, and academic institutions. Spending time at such places can enhance a career and be very rewarding. Do not be afraid to step out of a law firm to get more international experience. Also, do not agonize over that decision; as long as you are building your career, it doesn't really matter where you get your experience.

I spent five years at my first law firm in Seattle and then in its Washington, D.C. offices. At about the four-and-a-half-year mark, it became clear that I wanted to spend more time in Greater China. Through my work with the China Committee of the ABA Section of International Law, I had gotten to know some of the people involved with the Asian Institute of International Financial Law (AIIFL) at Hong Kong University's (HKU) Faculty of Law. AIIFL offered me a chance to become a Fellow and spend time at HKU. I really did not want to leave my first firm, but I decided that it was necessary in order to get more on-the-ground exposure in Greater China. I spent about two years traveling between Washington, D.C. and Hong Kong as an AIIFL Fellow. At AIIFL, among other things, I was able to work on research projects involving China's securities markets, publish China-related law review articles, and teach a few classes. I also participated in the 2003 Sino-U.S. Legal Exchange Program sponsored by the U.S. Department of Commerce and China's Ministry of Commerce. Most important, I got to spend a lot of time in China, and that was the best learning experience of all. I enjoyed my time at AIIFL, but I knew that at some point I'd have to return to the United States. You should keep building your contacts network, because you never know when you're going to need it.

F. Networking, Associations, and Branding

As a young lawyer, you should get involved in bar associations and community groups; they offer opportunities to speak, publish, and learn. These groups can also offer exposure to different cultures and business environments and provide valuable contacts around the world. In addition, these groups provide a way for lawyers to give back to their communities.

One of the best decisions I ever made was to become active in the ABA Section of International Law. I joined the Section because it was one of the few bar associations with a China-focused committee. My first step in joining the China Committee was contacting the then-chair, Jim Zimmerman, and asking how I could help with the committee's activities. Jim asked me to work with the committee's listserv and website. Soon after, I was asked to join the China Committee as a vice chair, where I continued to manage the Committee's website, started a working group on China's electronic commerce regulations, planned programs at Section events, and wrote the committee's year-in-review articles.

Without Jim's encouragement, I would not have been able to become active in the Section of International Law. I have found that the Section is different from many other bar associations, because most of our leaders are open and encouraging to young lawyers, and we operate, for the most part, as a meritocracy. The Section enables young lawyers to be as involved as they wish to be, on their own schedule. It has been a wonderful platform on which to build my brand.

As a young lawyer, you should also build your brand by taking on speaking and writing opportunities. One of the best decisions I made as a first-year associate with my first firm was to partner with the Seattle office of the U.S. Department of Commerce on a series of talks about the implications of the European Union's adoption of the Euro. Through these presentations I was able to meet current and potential clients, demonstrate an expertise, and generate good public relations for my firm. I was also able to publish several law review articles on China-related topics, each of which helped build my brand.

In August 2011, I became the youngest chair in Section history. I owe much to those who preceded me as chair and those who will follow, as well as the many members and leaders I have met along the way. They are not just my colleagues; they are friends. We share a common admiration for the Section of International Law and its mission to further the just implementation of the rule of law around the world. We strive to put out programs, publications, projects, and policies that enhance the practical skills of Section members.

The Section is a special place—we have members from more than 90 countries, and from a wide range of practice areas. Section leaders are always willing to share their experience and expertise. It is exactly the kind of organization that presents unique opportunities to build a "brand" to its members.

I joined my current firm in mid-2011—I joined the firm whose managing partner is another former chair of the Section. We have the Section in our firm DNA.

G. Conclusion

I hope that this overview has been helpful, and I know that some parts may be more relevant than others, based on the particular reader's ambitions. You should view my experience in such a light and feel free to determine whether my guidance should affect your own career development. Put another way, my experience is illustrative, and you should make up your own mind about how to develop your career.

I hope that you take away from this chapter an understanding that an international legal career is what one makes of it; you should take ownership of your destiny and challenge yourself to build the career you want. A final piece of advice and a request: being a lawyer is a serious job, involving long hours, demanding clients, and serious issues, but the job should be fun (or at least parts of it). So, while you should take your job and work product seriously, consider taking yourself a little less seriously.

Part 3

Rule of Law

An International Judge in Kosovo 10

by Hon. Marilyn J. Kaman

A. Introduction

My career in international law began unexpectedly. As I sat at in my office as a state-court trial judge in Hennepin County, Minnesota, a succinct e-mail appeared on my computer, from federal Judge Jack Tunheim, who had recently returned from Kosovo and who had been instrumental in rebuilding the judiciary in Kosovo after the 1999 conflict ended. The e-mail sent to all Minnesota state-court trial judges asked, "Would any Minnesota trial judge be interested in serving as an International Judge in Kosovo?" and contained the following announcement:

Field Mission Vacancy Notice

Field Mission Vacancy Notice
EXTERNAL/INTERNAL
Vacancy #: MIK/01-010-second issue Deadline: 21 March 2002 Post Title: International Judge Post Level: P-5/D-1 Location: Pristina, Kosovo Duties and Responsibilities: Under the overall supervision of the Director of the Department of Justice, the incumbent serves as an international judge in one of the five District Courts in Kosovo or in the Supreme Court of Kosovo, based in Pristina. In this role, the incumbent shall: Select, with a view to investigate or adjudicate, serious criminal cases within the jurisdiction of the courts of their assignment, including cases of genocide, war crimes, organized crime, murder, terrorism, ethnically motivated offences, trafficking in drugs and human beings, and smuggling of weapons and ammunition. Provide legal support and advice to the Department of Justice on criminal legal issues and the application of international human rights standards in Kosovo. Assist in UNMIK's overall efforts of strengthening the judiciary and establishing the rule of law in Kosovo. Participate and promotes institutional- and capacity-building efforts by UNMIK of the Kosovo judiciary at both the regional and provincial level. Perform any other duties that fall within the jurisdiction of judges as set out in the applicable law and UNMIK Regulations. Qualifications: Advanced university degree in law from a recognized university. Minimum of 20 years of relevant experience including 10 years handling criminal law cases as a professional judge in a court equivalent to the District Court in Kosovo or higher. Knowledge of the civil law system and/or the applicable law in Kosovo preferred. Familiarity with international human rights standards and legal principles.

The notice seemed clear enough. It called for a judge who could adjudicate criminal cases and provide support on criminal legal issues. The qualifications seemed to be tailor-made to my own professional experience.

I first entered the field of criminal law as a public defender in Hennepin County, Minnesota, which handles a greater volume of criminal cases than any other county in the state. By the time of my appointment to the district court bench six years later, I had tried dozens of jury cases and understood trial practice. This experience in criminal cases was reinforced by 12 years as a state-court trial judge, during which time I had encountered virtually every criminal case type within Minnesota's Criminal Code. Implicit in the notice also was a willingness to travel and to encounter the unknown. With my travel and education in the former Soviet Union in 1971, another piece of the puzzle was in place. By answering that e-mail, my career in international law was launched. My application (and the application of three other Minnesota trial court judges) was accepted. On November 17, 2002, I boarded a plane for Kosovo and became a participant in the post-war reconstruction process.

B. United Nations Mission in Kosovo

1. Some Background

The social fabric of Kosovo was torn apart by the region's ethnic strife during the 1980s and the 1990s. The conflict, between the Kosovar Serbs and Kosovar Albanians, dates back to the year 1389, with an Ottoman Empire victory at Kosovo Polje/Fushe Kosove, on the outskirts of present-day Pristina. With the death of Yugoslav President Josef Tito in 1980, the uneasy truce keeping the republics of Yugoslavia together—as well as ethnic rivalries—unraveled. Serbian leader Slobodan Milosevic rallied ethnic Serbs at Kosovo Polje/Fushe Kosove in 1987 by declaring, "No one should dare to beat you!" During the 1990s, Kosovar Albanian judges and police were dismissed from their posts, and schools for Kosovar Albanian children were closed.

A campaign to expel the Kosovar Albanian population from Kosovo was implemented. Newspapers across the world carried pictures of the forced exodus. NATO intervened on March 23, 1999, and the conflict ended 87 days later. On June 10, 1999, the United Nations Mission in Kosovo (UNMIK) was created by UN Security Council Resolution 1244. UNMIK's mandate was to act as the interim and transitional civilian administration for the region. Part of that mandate would be to maintain civil law and order, including establishment of the rule of law.

In 2000, UNMIK asked international judges and prosecutors to participate in Kosovo's judicial processes in order to ensure the independence and impartiality of the judiciary and the proper administration of justice. The continuing distrust of one ethnicity toward the other adversely affecting trial outcomes after June 1999 required this action.

2. Broadening Professional Knowledge and Expertise

The role of a judge in Kosovo, as I experienced it, was different from that of a state-court trial judge in the United States. The judicial system in Kosovo had its origins in the European civil law system (a new Criminal Code and Code of Criminal Procedure have since been adopted, modifying Kosovo's long-standing legal system). In addition to being a trial judge, I was called on to be an investigative judge, assuming a quasi-prosecutorial role by investigating crimes that had occurred and questioning witnesses and possible suspects.

The Field Vacancy Notice was accurate in the cases assigned to International Judges: war crimes, organized crime, murder, terrorism, ethnically motivated offenses, trafficking in drugs and human beings, and smuggling of weapons and ammunition. While in Kosovo, in addition to investigative hearings, I either was a presiding judge or panel judge on three trial panels. The war crimes case involved a defendant of Montenegrin origin accused of committing crimes against Kosovar Albanians in villages of the Pec/Peje during 1998 and 1999. Trial began in late January 2003 and concluded on June 26, 2003. The trial panel of three judges (two international judges and one professional Kosovar judge) found the defendant guilty of 7 counts of war crimes and acquitted him of 23 counts of war crimes. The second lengthy case involved charges of murder against two Kosovar Albanians accused of killing another Kosovar Albanian man for allegedly collaborating with Serbian authorities. The killing occurred on February 18, 1998 (before recognition of the existence of an internal conflict in

Kosovo). The trial panel of five judges (International Presiding Judge, professional Kosovar judge, three lay judges) convicted one defendant and acquitted the other.

The work to be done required not only learning the civil law system, but also integrating and applying several bodies of law as well: the Criminal Code for the Socialist Federal Republic of Yugoslavia, the Criminal Procedural Code for SFRY, the Serbian Criminal Code of 1989 (selected articles), the Kosovo Criminal Code, the Kosovo Code of Minor Offenses, international treaties, and principles of international law and international human rights.

For the next nine months as an International Judge in Kosovo, I delved into investigations, heard trials, and researched the applicable law. The process of judging in a civil law context sometimes required putting aside my common law approach to legal issues. What at first appeared to require a certain result, upon further examination called for a different result or approach. In short, my experience was a legal education by immersion that has greatly expanded my professional knowledge and expertise.

3. Professional and Personal Challenges

The professional and personal challenges that most quickly come to mind are summed up with the words *cold* and *intimidation.* The sheer cold of living without heat and electricity much of the day made an impression even on this hardy Minnesotan. Intimidation was a real message sent to both the international and the local Kosovar judges, by those who do not want the rule of law to prevail in Kosovo.

a. The Cold

Journal entry, February 18, 2003:

> It was cold in court today. We didn't have electricity for much of the session. We could see our breath in the courtroom. Luckily I put on an ankle-length skirt when I got dressed this morning. While listening to the testimony in the courtroom,
>
> I looked down at my legs, and realized that underneath my skirt was my long wool underwear that I have been using as pajamas. My down coat was draped over my legs. I looked at

the defendant, and he looked cold and forlorn. The witnesses who came to testify also looked cold and forlorn.

Two of my trial cases extended over a period of months and involved some thorny legal issues (war crimes prosecution). That being said, what would have been routine case-processing issues at home became hurdles to overcome: Would the witnesses in the outlying villages receive their subpoenas on time? Would any witnesses show up for court today? How could we contact village witnesses and tell them we were running behind? Was there any money with which to pay the witness fee? Would the court's backup generator work, or not? If not, how long would the court recorder's laptop function without electricity? Would the courthouse telephone land lines function on any given day? How cold should the courtroom be, before court is cancelled?

I am routinely asked what kinds of cases I heard, as well as the volume of my caseload. "Was it one case per day? One case per week? Do you mean you only tried three cases and you were in Kosovo for over seven months?" People are polite, but incredulous. The Field Mission Vacancy Notice did not draw attention to the word *mission*. Being "in mission" means doing without the conveniences taken for granted at home, such as reliable heat, light, and communication means. By Minnesota standards, the winter in Kosovo was not cold—the coldest temperature was in the 20s Fahrenheit. Without reliable electricity in Kosovo, however, that mild winter became very cold indeed. The sheer cold affected the way we did our work, as well as the way we lived.

b. Intimidation

As I drove to work in Kosovo on January 23, 2003, I approached the parking lot and saw yellow "Police Line Do Not Cross" tape extending around the perimeter of my building. A rocket-propelled grenade had been fired the night before into the Regional Police Headquarters in Pec/Peje, Kosovo. This building housed offices of all Pec/Peje international judges, international prosecutors, international interpreters, UN support staff, and international civilian police. About one week later, a Kosovar Albanian judge was severely beaten outside his home in

Prizren by persons unknown. One theory regarding the first incident is that displeasure was being expressed for a verdict rendered in December by my international colleague from Uganda. One theory regarding the second incident is that the local judge was too enthusiastic in his support of the prosecution of certain criminal elements.

Whatever the cause, the intended effect was clear: to create a climate of fear affecting judicial decision making. Once fear enters the equation, a judicial outcome can be dictated by politically or personally expedient considerations. While I was in Kosovo, two armed bodyguards accompanied me wherever I went. My Kosovar judicial colleagues did not have any protection. I often put myself in their shoes: Would I be able to make the correct decision, without protection and in a society filled with ethnic distrust, intimidation, and fear? It was not an easy question to ask myself. It is even more difficult to come up with an answer.

The cold and intimidation were only two of the challenges faced while I was in Kosovo. Yet, each challenge also was an opportunity for learning, both professional and personal.

C. Your Own Career in International Law

My mission to Kosovo ended in June 2003 at the end of my leave of absence and return to work as a state-court trial judge. In a real sense, however, my career in international law was just beginning. If you are considering a career in international law, the following sections provide some suggestions for you.

1. Career or Calling?

The word *career* most often calls up the connotation of a full-time occupation, established early in one's professional life. I now know that this one definition is not controlling and, in fact, may be a definition that, if adhered to, limits one's professional experience and opportunity. It may be better to note the dictionary definition of *career:* "a profession for which one trains and which is undertaken as a permanent calling" (Merriam-Webster). You can begin your career either while you are in law school, early thereafter, or sometime later in your professional career. The timing doesn't matter. What does matter is that if you are interested in international law, you should begin with the activity or subject matter that interests you. I have done reading, audited law school courses, joined professional organizations focusing on international law, written articles, and traveled as a delegation member to foreign countries. Through these activities, I consider myself to have a permanent calling in international law, one to which I am committed and about which I am most excited.

2. Legal Education

As is clear from what I have written, my legal education in international law developed backward. Instead of learning international law in advance, I learned by immersion once on the ground. It was a challenging process to learn, assimilate, and apply a new body of law all at once. On this issue, I would recommend learning ahead of time and getting all of the knowledge that you can.

If you are in law school, this means taking advantage of whatever international law courses your school has to offer. Take the introductory course in international law, and then follow up with courses in international criminal law, international humanitarian law, international human rights law, and advanced seminars on these subjects. Learn all you can about the UN, its history, programs, and international law initiatives. If comparative law courses are offered, take them. The more you know about major legal systems, adherence to treaties, and their implementation, the better trained you will be.

You also should not overlook the obvious: If you want to work in the arena of international criminal law, you should develop a solid foundation of litigation experience and criminal law expertise. This includes criminal law, criminal procedure, and evidence (beginning and advanced). Good oral and written advocacy skills are essential, and experience in moot court competition would be a definite asset. Finally, if your school offers legal advice clinics where you can appear in court (under the supervision of licensed attorneys) representing actual clients, you should consider enrolling in these clinics. Responding to the needs of clients, researching their legal problems, and finding solutions is far different from reading about it in textbooks. It is also excellent preparation for deciphering criminal issues in a litigation context in the future.

3. The Internet

Opportunities abound for careers in international law, both at home and abroad. If you are focusing on international court opportunities, each court has a website that will have "Job Recruitment" and/or internship opportunities. See the following court websites:

- The International Criminal Court (ICC) is an independent, permanent court that tries persons accused of the most serious crimes of international concern, namely genocide, crimes against humanity, and war crimes. The ICC is based on a treaty, joined by 104 countries. http://www.icc-cpi.int/
- The International Criminal Tribunal for the former Yugoslavia (ICTY) was established in 1993 in response to the threat to international peace and security, with the authority to prosecute and try grave breaches of the Geneva Conventions, genocide, and crimes against humanity; it currently is under a completion strategy targeted for 2010. http://www.un.org/icty/
- The International Criminal Tribunal for Rwanda (ICTR) was created in 1994 to prosecute persons responsible for genocide and other serious violations of international humanitarian law committed within Rwanda, as well as prosecution of Rwandan citizens committing crimes within neighboring states during the relevant period. http://69.94.11.53/default.htm
- The Extraordinary Chambers in the Courts of Cambodia was established in 2001 by a vote of the Cambodian National Assembly that enacted a law to create a court to try serious crimes committed during the Khmer Rouge regime from 1975 to 1979. This court is officially called the Extraordinary Chambers in the Courts of Cambodia for the Prosecution of Crimes Committed during the Period of Democratic Kampuchea (Extraordinary Chambers or ECCC). This special new court was created by the government of Cambodia and the UN, and will apply international standards. http://www.eccc.gov.kh/english/default.aspx
- A Special Tribunal for Lebanon was established in November 2006 by the UN Security Council, which voted to establish a special tribunal to investigate the assassination of Rafik Hariri in 2005.

- The Office of the High Representative is an ad hoc international institution responsible for overseeing implementation of civilian aspects of the accord ending the war in Bosnia and Herzegovina, and under its auspices a War Crimes Chamber is operated. http://www.ohr.int/

4. Networking

Upon my return from Kosovo, I promptly flew to San Francisco for the ABA Annual Meeting and joined the Section of International Law. My initial focus was the UN International Institutions Committee. From that, I have gone on to become a deputy editor of *International Law News* and co-chair of the International Criminal Law Committee, and I have taken International Legal Exchange (ILEX) trips to The Hague, Ghana, Liberia, and Sierra Leone. The ABA Section of International Law has committees that will be of interest to you. By not only joining but actively participating in these committees, you will continue to learn new developments in international law and will meet the leaders in their respective fields.

Moreover, internships are sometimes available on a short-term basis, during which time you will be able to perform substantive legal work and gain direct practical experience. The internships may be unpaid and are generally from four to six months. The International Criminal Court, for example, has both Internship Placements and Visiting Professional Placements, depending on the stage of your career. By trying one of these short-term internships, you can gain direct experience while determining whether a career in international law is right for you.

If you are a state-court trial judge, determine whether your district has a judicial leave of absence policy. I had the good fortune to go to Kosovo because our Chief Justice, Governor, and district Chief Judges jointly implemented a judicial leave policy (without pay) for endeavors such as this. If your judicial district does not have a policy permitting you to take an unpaid leave of absence from your judicial duties, it would be a project worth pursuing. As an international judge, you will find your professional horizons broadened and personal insights gained, while you foster the rule of law abroad.

5. Adaptability and Resilience

Doing the work of an international judge and living abroad requires a certain resilience and adaptability. If romantic notions come to mind, the reality is that this field requires a lot of hard work, under suboptimal conditions, and focuses on crimes that are some of the most horrific imagined. Yet what the work required of me is also what nourished me. Sitting with my colleagues in a small and bare courtroom in Kosovo, with only two desks, essential staff, a couple of guards, and counsel, it nevertheless was clear to me that this work was important to the world at large. It was tremendously satisfying to model the rule of law for the defendant, the victims, and the Kosovo judges and lawyers watching this process unfold. Working with my UN colleagues was an eminently gratifying experience, and one that has made a permanent impression on me.

D. Conclusion

After I returned home, I was asked what my experience in Kosovo was like. Here is my answer: Think of an adjective, any adjective at all. Whatever the adjective is, it likely applies to my experience in Kosovo. However, from my standpoint, the final adjective would have to be *extraordinary*. Being an International Judge in Kosovo was simply an extraordinary experience, fundamentally affecting my perspective on life and the law. If you are considering a career in international law, I highly encourage you to pursue this as your career calling.

The Journey of a Private Practitioner Who Became an International Rule of Law Attorney

11

by Mary Noel Pepys

A. The Journey

Fifteen years after graduating from law school, and having served as a government attorney in Washington, D.C. and a private practitioner in San Francisco, I decided in 1993 to embark on an unknown venture with the idealistic fervor of a Peace Corps volunteer. Despite my established professional life, lucrative income, and being in my forties, I volunteered for the newly created non-profit ABA Central European and Eurasian Law Initiative (CEELI), a technical legal assistance provider created in 1990 by the ABA Section of International Law, which is more fully described on page xxvii.

As the Berlin Wall was being dismantled, signifying the demise of communism, CEELI was created to support the efforts of former communist countries to build their democracies and market-based economies. These countries were faced with the daunting task of creating new legal systems, drafting new constitutions for their recently obtained independence, and writing a myriad of laws that embraced democratic principles and private commerce. The ABA believed that by sending experienced American attorneys to serve as liaisons to live and work *pro bono* in Central and Eastern Europe and the former Soviet Union for an extended period of time, significant U.S. legal assistance could be provided to enhance the judiciary, legal profession, and legal education of these countries.

I volunteered with CEELI because I wanted to participate in the birthing process of democracy. I was intrigued with the prospect of working with lawyers and judges who lived under a political system that preached the supremacy of the State, and seemingly overnight changed its sermon to extol the virtues of democracy, of genuine public participation in government. I was curious to see how millions of citizens accustomed to State guarantees of housing, food, employment, medical care, and even vacations could suddenly assume the burdens of freedom, taking responsibility for their own lives.

After months of preparation and temporarily closing my office as a solo practitioner, I arrived in Sofia, Bulgaria, filled with hopes and expectations. What I saw were gray skies, dull and dilapidated buildings, potholes large enough to sink trucks, and horrific emissions from buses and factories. Winter had set in, but the heating, which was central to the city, had not been turned on. The heat was turned on when the city bureaucrats decided to turn it on, and not a minute before. Once turned on, it was kept on 24 hours a day until spring. The only way I could regulate the heat in my apartment was to open the windows—even during snowstorms.

And I wasn't getting paid for this?

But I, like scores of other volunteers, did not join CEELI for the comforts of home; otherwise, we would not have left. We joined as short-term volunteers to make a difference in the lives of others. Many of us continued with CEELI because our work to enhance the rule of law in former communist countries was fascinating. In the beginning, CEELI liaisons had to commit to six months, but many remained for a year and some even two. I was a CEELI liaison for five years, living one year each in Bulgaria, Latvia, and Slovakia and the remaining two years in Ukraine, Kazakhstan, and Croatia.

Why did I work *pro bono* for five years, a financially precarious situation?

Imagine working in a former communist country and having your first meeting of the day with the chief justice of the Supreme Court. With the assistance of a translator, you discuss ways in which the governance structure of the judicial branch can be enhanced to ensure the independence of the courts. Transitioning from a history of subservience to the State, judges need not only to develop a structure that guarantees their independence, but also to learn how to assert their judicial prerogative.

The meeting ends and you, along with your translator, walk to the national bar association office where a group of young lawyers are interested in strengthening their legal skills. Since private practice is a relatively new concept in many former communist countries, these young lawyers want to learn best practices from experienced lawyers around the world. They pepper you with questions and are eager to learn from your expertise. You agree to meet again before heading off to your last meeting.

The legal affairs committee of Parliament wants to draft a new law on legal education. Now that privatization is becoming an economic reality, the curriculum at law schools must be revised to incorporate the new laws pertaining to private property and a market-based economy. The parliamentarians with whom you meet are interested in obtaining curricula from a variety of American law schools.

This was a typical day in my life as a CEELI liaison.

Essentially, I provided technical assistance in developing judicial training centers, judges' associations, bar associations, and women legal professional associations; enhanced legal education curricula and teaching instruction; supported legal publications by bar associations and law faculties; developed codes of ethics and training on ethics; assisted legal professional non-governmental organizations to become self-sufficient by engaging directors and staff in governance and fundraising activities; and conducted numerous international workshops, conferences, and study trips for legal professionals.

Following my work with CEELI, I returned to San Francisco and became a consultant to other rule of law technical assistance providers, which has given me the opportunity to work short-term in such disparate countries as Mongolia, Papua New Guinea, Lebanon, Nepal, and Algeria as well as 36 other countries.

The lure of living abroad enticed me once again, and in 2008 I moved to Afghanistan to work as the justice adviser for the Department of State Bureau of International Narcotics and Law Enforcement Affairs, more fully described on page 125, whose mission is to help nations establish a capable and accountable criminal justice sector. I was responsible for managing two nationwide criminal justice development programs in Afghanistan focused on institutional capacity building, training, and mentoring: (1) the Justice Sector Support Program (JSSP), currently with over 48 American rule of law attorneys to work with the Ministry of Justice, Attorney General's Office, Supreme Court, and Ministry of Women's Affairs, and (2) the Corrections System Support Program (CSSP), currently with over 70 American corrections advisers to work with the Afghan Central Prison Directorate and the Afghan Juvenile Rehabilitation Directorate to develop a safe, secure, and humane Afghan corrections system.

All of my work was conducted out of the confines of the U.S. Embassy compound in Kabul, where I lived in a "hooch," a 10" x 12" shipping container, for 18 months. During this time I never walked a street in Kabul, never went into any shop or museum, never bought local food or clothes or visited anyone's home. I went to meetings in Kabul's governmental buildings and at the JSSP and CSSP compounds, where American advisers were also confined to a limited fortified space, wearing a flak jacket and sometimes a helmet. I was transported by armored vehicles, often protected by men with M-4s, and flew over the countryside to attend events with armed guards as flight attendants.

We worked together to enhance the lives of the Afghan legal community. Prosecutors and judges in some provinces are illiterate, while others have the equivalent of a high-school education. With the assistance of other rule of law attorneys, we developed, through comprehensive training, a skilled cadre of justice sector professionals who are committed to serving Afghanistan.

While my international rule of law experiences have been challenging and, indeed, very exciting, they are not unique. As I work around the world, I always meet other lawyers who have also fallen under the spell of international rule of law work and have taken a rain check in returning to their previous U.S. legal work. Although rule of law attorneys work in countries under vastly different circumstances and with vastly different political and legal systems, the nature of the work is similar, as the principles of judicial independence, legal profession, legal education, and human rights are international and transcend geographic borders.

B. The Substantive Work of International Rule of Law Attorneys

The work of an international rule of law attorney is varied and includes writing constitutions, drafting laws incorporating democratic standards and market-based economic principles, developing self-sustaining government institutions, and enhancing the quality of professionals in the legal and judicial sectors.

Essentially the work ensures that the basic principles of protection of the human rights of citizens, equal treatment of all individuals before the law, and a predictable legal system with fair, transparent, and effective judicial institutions are pursued. Protecting citizens against the arbitrary use of state authority in countries with weak or newly emerging democratic traditions, where laws are not fair or fairly applied, and where judicial independence is compromised, is the foremost objective of international rule of law attorneys.

Substantive areas in which international rule of law attorneys practice are:

Judicial Reform
Increasing the independence of the judicial systems by improving the administration, accountability, and transparency of the courts and enhancing the competency, impartiality, and integrity of judges. In a democracy based on the rule of law, every citizen is entitled to a fair and timely hearing by an independent and impartial judicial tribunal conducted according to the due process of law. However, in many developing countries, judges are not impartial, nor are they committed to applying the law justly. Instead, they are dependent on political or other external factors, often because their appointment was based on their ideology rather than their competency. Since an independent judiciary is the cornerstone of a democracy based on the rule of law, this area is one of the highest priorities of rule of law assistance.

Legal Profession Reform
Increasing the competency of the legal profession by developing voluntary bar associations to improve the education and ethics of attorneys, thereby enhancing their skills to serve as advocates for and

protectors of the rule of law; developing and administering bar examinations; developing codes of legal ethics; and enhancing continuing legal education programs to ensure adequate mastery of existing and newly enacted laws.

Legal Education Reform

Assisting law schools to enhance their curricula by integrating substantive courses based on new laws and by incorporating practice-based legal education programs, such as moot court competitions, externship programs, *pro bono* clinics, and advocacy skills courses, and by improving the skills of law professors by training them on modern adult-teaching techniques.

Criminal Law Reform

Reforming key criminal law legislation, such as criminal procedure codes, and drafting and implementing modern criminal justice legislation to more effectively combat crimes such as human trafficking, money laundering, and cybercrime; and training criminal justice professionals, including police, prosecutors, investigators, and defense attorneys.

Access to Justice

Establishing public defender programs as well as legal aid and law school clinics, and supporting justice system reforms that increase access to the courts.

Alternative Dispute Resolutions

Providing alternatives to formal court processes, such as introducing mediation and arbitration or enhancing existing customary traditional and informal justice processes, particularly in countries where corruption is endemic or where court delays are so significant that justice is often denied.

Human Rights and Post-Conflict

Increasing awareness of international human rights standards and humanitarian law, documenting human rights abuses, and training legal professionals to seek redress for human rights violations in both domestic and regional/international courts.

Anti-Corruption and Public Integrity
Combating corruption and increasing transparency and accountability by developing and implementing public integrity standards, freedom of information laws, and national anti-corruption action plans; educating the public about the corrosive impact of corruption on society and the economy; and encouraging the public to combat corruption through mechanisms such as anonymous hotlines.

Gender Issues
Educating governmental officials concerning the importance of women's rights issues and assisting the government and non-governmental organizations to address domestic violence, human trafficking, sexual harassment in the workplace, and widespread gender-based violence (including systematic rape) in conflict and post-conflict situations.

Civic Education
Promoting a rule of law culture through civic education campaigns on the rule of law and citizens' rights.

Institution Building
Creating and supporting the organizational development and sustainability of indigenous institutions that actively promote democratic reforms, such as law student organizations, bar associations, and judicial training centers.

In addition to knowing the substantive areas of rule of law assistance, international rule of law attorneys must be cognizant of and responsive to the needs and priorities of the local institutions in the countries where they work. Rather than insist on implementing the norms of developed countries, particularly the United States, attorneys must employ a consultative approach to providing technical assistance by working closely with local experts. Given that many of the countries where rule of law assistance is provided operate under a civil law system, the advice and technical assistance given by attorneys must be relevant to the unique issues of a civil law system. The U.S. legal system is discussed only when comparative models are requested or, in some cases, where facets of the comon law system, e.g., adversarial proceedings or jury trials in civil cases, may be used as a model in judicial reform. To be truly successful, however, rule of law attorneys must be sensitive to and properly address the culture and customs of the country and individual practices.

C. U.S. Government Bodies and International Organizations Supporting Rule of Law Technical Legal Assistance

The principal U.S. government funder for rule of law technical assistance is the U.S. Agency for International Development, which provides assistance to countries engaging in democratic reforms and conflict prevention. The U.S. Department of State and the U.S. Department of Justice also provide significant rule of law technical assistance, while the U.S. Department of Defense has recently become involved in supporting the rule of law, given the wars in Iraq and Afghanistan. The two major international organizations supporting rule of law technical legal assistance are The World Bank and the United Nations. The Asia Development Bank, Inter-American Development Bank, and African Development Bank are regional, multilateral development finance institutions, which promote, through loans and grants, democratic reform, economic and social development, and modernization of the state.

1. U.S. Agency for International Development (USAID)

USAID's programs are grounded on the premise that the rule of law is the cornerstone for all other elements of democracy. A free and fair political system, protection of human rights, a vibrant civil society, public confidence in the police and the courts, and economic development all depend on accountable governments, fair and accessible application of the law, and respect for international human rights standards. In post-conflict settings, reestablishing the rule of law is the first step in the rebuilding process. Establishing peace and security and rebuilding justice institutions help to develop the necessary climate for reconciliation, public confidence, and subsequent economic growth.

USAID's efforts to enhance the rule of law fosters five essential elements: (1) Order and Security—rule of law cannot flourish when public order breaks down and citizens fear for their safety; (2) Legitimacy—laws are legitimate when they represent societal consensus; (3) Checks and Balances—rule of law depends on a separation of governmental powers; (4) Fairness—the poor and disadvantaged, including women, must be empowered by the equal application of the law, procedural fairness, protection of human rights and civil liberties, and access to justice; and (5) Effective Application—without consistent enforcement and application for all citizens and other inhabitants, there can be no rule of law.

2. U.S. Department of State

The other major U.S. government funder for rule of law technical assistance is the U.S. Department of State Bureau of International Narcotics and Law Enforcement Affairs (INL), which serves as the lead U.S. government agency on international criminal justice sector reform. Its mission is to minimize the impact of international crime and illegal drugs on the United States, its citizens, and partner nations by providing effective foreign assistance and fostering global cooperation. Its criminal justice reform programs help to strengthen justice sector institutions in order to promote peace and security, good governance, and the rule of law, and cover a diverse range of initiatives, including working with law enforcement officers, correction officials, court employees, and judges. Its anti-narcotics programs focus on building interdiction capabilities, eradication, sustainable alternative development, and reducing drug use. Its transnational crime program seeks to minimize the impact of transnational crime and criminal networks on the United States and its allies through enhanced international cooperation and foreign assistance. INL employs roughly 7,000 people (including civil servants, foreign service officers, contractors, and local hires) with programs in more than 70 countries. INL implements its programs through: (1) funding to federal, state, and local agencies; (2) contracts with individuals and private firms chosen through a competitive process; (3) grants to non-profits and universities; and (4) contributions and secondments to multilateral organizations.

3. U.S. Department of Justice (DOJ)

DOJ is engaged in over 60 countries on rule of law work developing professional and accountable law enforcement institutions. Through the International Criminal Investigative Training Assistance Program (ICITAP), DOJ assists foreign governments by providing professional law enforcement services based on democratic principles respecting human rights, combating corruption, and reducing the threat of transnational crimes and terrorism. Through the Office of Overseas Prosecutorial Development, Assistance and Training (OPDAT), DOJ develops and administers technical assistance designed to enhance the capabilities of foreign justice system institutions and their law enforcement personnel to effectively combat terrorism, trafficking in persons, organized crime, corruption, and financial crimes.

4. U.S. Department of Defense (DOD)

DOD assists other U.S. government agencies in planning and executing reconstruction and stabilization efforts toward strengthening governance and the rule of law. DOD's rule of law operations are particularly important following major ground combat operations when the governance of society is disrupted by combat, requiring order to be restored to the civilian population. DOD's emphasis on the rule of law is to foster security and stability for the civilian population by supporting effective and fair administration and enforcement of justice. In security and counterinsurgency operations that pertain to promoting the rule of law in Iraq and Afghanistan, DOD collaborates closely with other U.S. government agencies. Judge advocates of the Judge Advocate General's Corps promote the rule of law by serving as: (1) legal advisers to commanders and their staff on rule of law issues, (2) mentors to judges and governmental officials, (3) drafters of host-nation laws and presidential decrees, and (4) facilitators at rule of law conferences.

U.S. Employment Procedures

All U.S. government positions are advertised on the website www.usajobs.com, while all U.S. government contract positions are listed on the website www.fedbizopps.com.

5. The World Bank

The World Bank provides significant rule of law funding in its overarching effort to reduce poverty. Over the past two decades, The World Bank has promoted adherence to the rule of law as a fundamental element of economic development and poverty reduction. The World Bank's justice sector work combines financial support, technical assistance, and research. Its portfolio comprises 36 projects investing $850 million that are solely dedicated to justice sector reform; an additional 388 investment lending projects in other sectors that include at least 10 percent of expenditure allocated to the rule of law or justice; and nearly one-third of The World Bank's development policy loans include law and justice policy actions. The World Bank's justice work focuses not only on the role of the justice sector in improving the commercial environment, but also on its role in governance and anti-corruption, as well as its role in ensuring fairness and equity in society especially for the poor and vulnerable. The World Bank has two specific programs for attorneys: the Legal Associates Program and the Legal Interns Program. They can be accessed at http://go.worldbank.org/SK9CKPG830.

6. United Nations

The UN is heavily involved in funding the rule of law in specific areas: justice, security, prison and penal reform, legal reform, constitution making, and transitional justice. The UN Rule of Law Coordination and Resource Group (Group) is responsible for the overall coordination and coherence of rule of law within the UN system. The Group is chaired by the Deputy Secretary-General and supported by its secretariat, the Rule of Law Unit. Members of the Group are the principals of the Department of Political Affairs, the Department of Peacekeeping Operations, Office of the High Commissioner for Human Rights, the Office of Legal Affairs, UN Development Programme, the Office of the UN High Commissioner for Refugees, the UN Children's Fund, the UN Entity for Gender Equality and the Empowerment of Women, and the UN Office on Drugs and Crime. The Group serves an important coordination function, while the operational role remains squarely with the individual UN entities listed above. The Group can be accessed at www.unrol.org.

D. Opportunities for International Rule of Law Attorneys

Rule of law technical assistance is carried out primarily by for-profit companies and non-profit organizations, many of which are listed below. One of the most effective methods for entering the increasingly competitive arena of international rule of law work, particularly for new attorneys who have little international work experience, is to obtain a volunteer position with the American Bar Association Rule of Law Initiative. Other opportunities also exist by working directly with the U.S. government, The World Bank, and the UN.

1. American Bar Association Rule of Law Initiative (ABA ROLI)

ABA ROLI is a non-profit program grounded in the belief that rule of law promotion is the most effective long-term antidote to the most pressing problems facing the world today, including poverty, conflict, corruption, and disregard for human rights. The ABA established the program in 2007 to consolidate its five overseas rule of law programs, including CEELI, which it created in 1990 after the fall of the Berlin Wall.

ABA ROLI implements legal reform programs in more than 40 countries in Africa, Asia, Europe and Eurasia, Latin America and the Caribbean, the Middle East and North Africa. ABA ROLI has more than 400 professional staff working in the United States and abroad, including a cadre of short- and long-term expatriate volunteers who, since the program's inception, have contributed more than $200 million in *pro bono* technical legal assistance.

The core principles that guide ABA ROLI's work are:

1. Employing a highly *consultative* approach to the delivery of technical assistance that is responsive to the requests and priorities of ABA ROLI's local partners;
2. Employing a *comparative* approach in providing technical legal assistance, with the U.S. legal system providing just one of several models that host country reformers can draw upon;
3. Providing technical assistance and advice that is *neutral* and *apolitical;*

4. Building local *capacity* by strengthening institutions in both the governmental and non-governmental sectors and by furthering the professional development of ABA ROLI's host country staff, many of whom become the next generation of leaders in their countries; and

5. Providing *thought leadership* in rule of law promotion that draws on ABA ROLI's extensive overseas field experience and on the resources and convening power of the ABA and its more than 400,000 members in the United States and abroad.

ABA ROLI places an emphasis on collaborative and sustainable efforts that build upon stakeholder consensus. ABA ROLI's local partners include judges, lawyers, bar associations, law schools, court administrators, legislatures, ministries of justice, human rights organizations, and civil society members.

While ABA ROLI implements its technical assistance programs in a wide array of substantive areas, including commercial and property law reform, its efforts are concentrated in the seven focal areas: (1) Access to Justice and Human Rights; (2) Anti-Corruption and Public Integrity; (3) Criminal Law Reform and Anti-Human Trafficking; (4) Judicial Reform; (5) Legal Education Reform and Civic Education; (6) Legal Profession Reform; and (7) Women's Rights.

ABA ROLI's overseas work is supported by legal research and assessments. The program conducts in-depth assessments of draft legislation at the request of host country partners, conducts legal research, produces resource guides on rule of law issues, and develops and implements a range of acclaimed assessment tools. ABA ROLI has conducted over 50 assessments in more than 20 countries using these tools, all of which are publicly available and are regularly relied upon by local reformers, technical assistance providers, international donors, and scholars. To date, ABA ROLI has developed the following assessment tools:

1. Judicial Reform Index
2. Legal Profession Reform Index
3. Prosecutorial Reform Index
4. Legal Education Reform Index
5. Access to Justice Assessment Tool

6. Detention Procedure Assessment Tool
7. HIV/AIDS Legal Assessment Tool
8. Human Trafficking Assessment Tool, based on the United Nations Anti-Human Trafficking Protocol to the United Nations Convention against Transnational Organized Crime
9. ICCPR Index, based on the United Nations International Covenant on Civil and Political Rights; and
10. CEDAW Assessment Tool, based on the Convention on the Elimination of All Forms of Discrimination against Women.

ABA ROLI's Pro Bono Legal Specialist Program offers qualified individuals the opportunity to volunteer their time and services overseas. For volunteer positions abroad, the ABA ROLI only considers professionals with a minimum of five years of relevant experience, a high level of energy and initiative, strong interpersonal skills, and relevant substantive legal expertise. International experience and foreign-language skills are preferred but not always required. Both short-term and long-term opportunities are available. www.abarol.org

In addition to ABA ROLI, there are numerous for-profit companies and non-profit organizations that receive funding to provide rule of law technical assistance. The ones listed below have provided their own description of their rule of law services, which is quoted below, and their website for more information and application for rule of law positions. There are other rule of law companies and organizations, not listed below, whose work is contracted in-country and managed by the field missions of USAID and other entities.

2. ABA-United Nations Development Programme (UNDP) International Legal Assistance Resource Center (ILRC)

The ILRC, created by the ABA Section of International Law in December 1999, provides a legal resource capability to serve UNDP's global governance programs and projects supporting legal reform and democratic institution building. The primary task of the ILRC is to assist UNDP and country offices to identify experts capable of providing legal advice on the drafting of legislation, judicial reform, building of legal institutions including professional groups and associations, and other legal dimensions of governance. In addition, the ILRC conducts assessments of draft and current legislation, gauging its compliance with international standards where appropriate, and provides substantive legal research. Technical legal assistance is also provided to other UN entities, such as UN Women and the UN Office on Drugs and Crime, and, more recently, the International Finance Corporation, a member of The World Bank Group. Lastly, the ILRC continues to expand its range of capabilities and is flexible in responding to the changing needs of these multilateral organizations and their local partners.

The ILRC provides technical assistance in a wide variety of areas, including reforming legal institutions and systems; establishing new access to justice mechanisms; building constitutional frameworks; supporting electoral bodies and drafting election laws; improving legislative drafting and parliamentary practices; restructuring public-sector regulations and processes; strengthening anti-corruption measures; sustaining decentralization measures and strengthening local institutions; developing independent lawyer associations; conducting legal education and judicial training; providing legal services and advice to indigent and marginalized populations; and evaluating UNDP projects and assisting with work plan development. www.ambar.org/ilrc

3. AMEX International (AMEX)

AMEX was founded in 1982 to provide specialized services to government agencies, international institutions, and corporations worldwide. These services include stimulating economic growth by improving the competitiveness of the private sector and by cultivating a sound and enabling policy and regulatory environment; enhancing democracy and improve governance through increased citizen participation and upholding the rule of law; and improving administrative and management capacity. The specific areas in AMEX's Democracy and Governance work encompass administrative law reform; civic education and human-rights advocacy; conflict mediation and resolution; strengthening judicial systems and legislative processes; institutional and human-resource capacity building; and project design, management, and evaluation. www.amexdc.com

4. Asia Foundation

The Asia Foundation's law programs support Asian efforts to protect the legal rights of vulnerable groups; strengthen dispute resolution processes; and reform dysfunctional laws, policies, institutions, and practices. People across Asia face systemic challenges in resolving their disputes, enforcing their rights, and accessing the benefits to which they are legally entitled. The Asia Foundation's approach to addressing these problems and to law programming is anchored in a nuanced understanding of how reform processes work, based on more than 50 years of on-the-ground experience in Asia. The Asia Foundation's law programs are informed by an analysis of the connections between the functions of the legal system and the broader processes of economic, social, and political change taking place in a given society. This analysis provides the Asia Foundation with an empirically grounded basis for designing targeted program interventions where the Asia Foundation sees clear potential for traction and results. www.asiafoundation.org

5. BlueLaw International (BlueLaw)

BlueLaw is an international development consulting firm providing technical services on rule of law, justice and security sector, and anticorruption reform programs. BlueLaw has active contracts with the Department of State, USAID, and other implementing donors in the key areas of defense, diplomacy, and development. With previous and ongoing work in more than 25 countries, BlueLaw is adept at implementing effective programs in fragile, conflict-affected, and post-conflict states. BlueLaw work is generally divided into three major practice areas: (1) Security and Justice, which focuses on rule of law (including work with judiciaries, courts, lawyers, bar associations, and national ministries), anticorruption, and "soft side" security sector reform; (2) Human Rights and Inclusive Development, which promotes legal reform and civic activity that help ensure full access to justice for groups that are often excluded or marginalized in everyday society, such as women, children, and persons with disabilities; and (3) Integrated Law Enforcement Development, which supports reform efforts of police, corrections, border, and maritime protection forces to improve internal organization, community engagement, and capacity to operate in a democratic system. www.bluelawinternational.com

6. Casals & Associates (Casals)

Casals, a DynCorp International company, is an international development firm specializing in solutions to social, institutional, and political challenges. Casals provides services in areas such as anti-corruption, rule of law, and democratic transition. Casals's primary clients are USAID and the U.S. Department of State. It implements development programming wherever solutions for transparent and effective government are needed. Taken as a whole, the DynCorp International family of companies designs and delivers services supporting defense, diplomacy, and international development activities around the world. Clients include the U.S. Department of State and the UN, which call upon DynCorp International to support them in all aspects of their operations, including aviation, logistics, platform support, contingency operations, training and mentoring, community stability, and the rule of law. www.casals.com and www.dyn-intl.com.

7. Checchi Consulting (Checchi)

Checchi has been a USAID implementing partner for nearly 40 years. The company has worked in more than 140 countries and has completed nearly 300 long-term technical assistance implementation contracts. Since launching one of the first international rule of law practices in the late 1980s, Checchi has successfully completed more than 40 major contracts and task orders aimed at strengthening the rule of law and judicial reform. Nearly all of these projects have been long-term, multi-component undertakings requiring strong management and leadership and the mobilization of large teams of international and local specialists. Currently, Checchi is implementing large rule of law projects in Asia, Eastern Europe, and Latin America. www.checchiconsulting.com

8. Chemonics International (Chemonics)

Chemonics is a Washington, D.C.-based consulting firm that implements USAID-funded development projects around the globe. It works in a range of technical sectors, including democracy and governance. In this sector, Chemonics seeks to build legal and policy frameworks, capacity of professionals, and citizen participation that breathe legitimacy and fairness into government and increase public confidence in government institutions. Chemonics has established legal frameworks for emerging and transitioning states, improved the professionalism of legal and judicial officers, and modernized courts and their administration. At the same time, Chemonics' projects have worked to fully involve civil society to build awareness and capacity to participate in promoting reform priorities. Underlying all aspects of Chemonics' approach to developing rule of law institutions is a customer-service orientation, wherein demand drives reform and Chemonics' work builds on domestic practices and concerns. www.chemonics.com.

9. Democracy International (DI)

DI is a registered small business that provides technical assistance, supplies analytical services, and implements projects for democracy and governance programs worldwide for USAID and other development partners. DI's core capabilities and principal focus are solely in international democracy and governance assistance. DI offers a range of rule of law development services, including expertise in justice-sector institutions, legal frameworks and law reform, law enforcement, legal training and professional development, and legal access and advocacy. To bolster program effectiveness and long-term sustainability, DI's approach emphasizes local ownership to ensure the development of local capacity and effective knowledge transfer. To this end, DI works to bolster the effectiveness of justice- and public-sector institutions to ensure transparency and accountability in the delivery of justice and respect for human rights. DI approaches rule of law projects in an interdisciplinary and participatory manner with a strong emphasis on overall democracy and governance development, sustainable and culturally adapted strategies, civil society engagement, and critical analysis. DI has extensive experience designing, implementing, and evaluating rule of law projects in all regions of the world. www. democracyinternational.com

10. Development Alternatives, Inc. (DAI)

DAI has implemented wide-ranging programs to promote the rule of law and human rights in countries as varied and complex as Iraq, Bangladesh, Pakistan, Afghanistan, Sudan, Zimbabwe, the Philippines, Timor-Leste, Vietnam, the Dominican Republic, and the Democratic Republic of Congo. DAI takes a holistic view of justice, placing the needs of the poor, disadvantaged, and vulnerable at the center. DAI works to strengthen formal justice institutions in stable environments, but also emphasizes access to justice in conflict and post-conflict countries working with customary, traditional, and religious informal systems. www.dai.com

11. Development Professionals Inc. (DPI)

DPI is a small, woman-owned business headquartered in Falls Church, Virginia. DPI is focused on rule of law development and is implementing projects in Europe, Eurasia, and Africa. DPI's projects include providing technical assistance to prosecutors in South Africa to prosecute gender-based violence cases. In Serbia, DPI is developing the skills of the misdemeanor courts' staff in court administration through the development of model courts. DPI has provided technical assistance and guidance to USAID in monitoring and evaluation, and in developing rule of law strategies in Bangladesh, Lebanon, Albania, and Azerbaijan. www.developmentpi.com

12. Development and Training Services, Inc. (dTS)

dTS is a strategic management consulting firm leading initiatives in social and economic development with a view to promoting equality and accountability. Since 2002, dTS has provided services in 61 countries across the world. dTS promotes gender equality and social inclusion within economic, social, and political development programs through research, assessments, strategic planning, technical assistance, training, and capacity building so that all individuals can contribute to and benefit from their countries' development. dTS has experience in providing its gender integration, monitoring and evaluation, and training services in the following sectors: economic growth, democracy and governance, natural resource management, environment, energy, health, and education. dTS also helps to increase access to justice for women, men and youth, and people with disabilities. www.onlinedts.com

13. East-West Management Institute, Inc. (EWMI)

EWMI was founded in 1988 as an independent, not-for-profit organization, which promotes the rule of law, civil society, and free market systems globally. EWMI provides training, technical expertise, and grants to foster sustainable reforms in government, business, and civil society. Working in partnership with grassroots groups, local governments, and international organizations, EWMI combines legal, civic, and economic initiatives to build just, prosperous, and democratic societies. EWMI's expertise includes judicial reform, legislative framework reform, court administration, anti-corruption and transparency, judicial and legal education, and access to justice. EWMI has implemented or is implementing rule of law projects in Albania, Bosnia, Bulgaria, Cambodia, Ecuador, Egypt, Georgia, Kosovo, Liberia, Montenegro, Romania, Russia, Serbia, and Sri Lanka. EWMI uses top experts in the legal reform area, in particular those with international experience in court administration, criminal justice reform, access to justice, and legal education. www.ewmi.org

14. Financial Markets International, Inc. (FMI)

FMI, founded in 1992, is an international law and economics consulting firm, specializing in helping emerging market countries achieve economic growth and development through reliance on market mechanisms, international best practices, and commercial law reform. FMI has worked in more than 30 countries for international donor agencies and private commercial clients and is well known for its work in developing securities markets, commodity futures markets, capital markets, and non-bank financial institutions. FMI's work also encompasses legal and regulatory reform projects, pension reform, banking, finance for small and medium enterprises, institutional development, strategic planning, management information systems, and education and training initiatives. www.fmi-inc.net

15. Freedom House

Freedom House is one of the oldest human rights organizations in the United States that promotes democracy and fundamental freedoms worldwide. Its annual surveys, including the Freedom in the World survey, include critical rule of law indicators when evaluating the state of freedom in all countries of the world. Additionally, Freedom House's projects support human rights defenders, including legal professionals and judges, to promote rule of law and to push their systems from within to address human rights abuses and undertake needed remedies and reforms. Freedom House projects combine training and strategic advice to defenders on human rights investigations, documentation, reporting, and litigation, with policy advocacy at the national, regional, and international levels. Freedom House works in some of the most repressive societies, but also in countries experiencing democratic breakthroughs or regression. www.freedomhouse.org

16. Global Rights

Global Rights is an international human rights organization that works side-by-side with local activists in Asia, Africa, and Latin America. Access to justice is the primary principle that connects Global Rights' programs and initiatives and builds its partners' capacity to use legal empowerment tools within formal and informal justice systems that best fit their context. Global Rights conducts grassroots legal education and helps implement paralegal training for communities that lack access to lawyers. Global Rights trains partners to document and monitor human rights abuses to develop advocacy campaigns to change a law or harmful practice. Global Rights' activities also include judicial monitoring, use of strategic litigation, and the use of regional and international mechanisms to pressure governments to change laws or practices. www.globalrights.org

17. Independent Development Law Organization (IDLO)

IDLO is an intergovernmental organization that promotes the rule of law by providing technical assistance and capacity building in governance and justice sector reform; economic growth and trade; and social development program areas. IDLO has established programs that focus on a wide range of rule of law themes, including legal empowerment of the poor, provision of legal services to vulnerable populations, and use of local and international law to mitigate the risks of global challenges, including climate change, HIV/AIDs, and human trafficking. Additionally, IDLO seeks to advance the knowledge base on the rule of law, and actively shares this information with and for the international development community. IDLO manages multi-donor portfolios of large, complex programs to implement multifaceted activities in such diverse countries as Afghanistan, Ecuador, Egypt, Ethiopia, Haiti, Indonesia, Kenya, Kyrgyzstan, Lebanon, Mexico, Nepal, Paraguay, Somalia, South Sudan, Tajikistan, Ukraine, and Vietnam. www.idlo.int

18. International Business & Technical Consultants, Inc. (IBTCI)

IBTCI was incorporated in 1987 and remains focused on meeting the development assistance needs of emerging markets and developing countries by offering functional expertise, regional experience, and a commitment to excellence in the practice areas of monitoring and evaluation; accountancy, integrity, and financial management; banking and non-bank financial markets; procurement reform; and sector development and competitiveness. IBTCI's rule of law work has included evaluations of country programs to determine whether they have met the objectives of rule of law strengthening and the sustainability of those efforts and has also implemented rule of law assessments to examine the opportunities and constraints related to the further development of rule of law in a country. IBTCI has conducted rule of law programs around the world, including in Armenia, Cambodia, and Kyrgyzstan. www.ibtci.com

19. International Commission of Jurists (ICJ)

The ICJ, founded in 1952 in West Berlin, Germany, is dedicated to the primacy, coherence, and implementation of international law and principles that advance human rights. The ICJ provides an impartial, objective, and authoritative legal approach to the protection and promotion of human rights through the rule of law. The ICJ provides legal expertise at both the international and national levels to ensure that developments in international law adhere to human rights principles and that international standards are implemented at the national level. www.icj.org

20. International Foundation for Electoral Systems (IFES)

IFES is a private, non-profit organization established in 1987 to support electoral and other democratic institutions in emerging, evolving, and experienced democracies. IFES engages in legal drafting, legislative review, and commentary pertaining to election laws, and capacity building of civil society organizations in the field of election law reform. www.ifes.org

21. International Law Institute (ILI)

ILI, founded as part of Georgetown University in 1955 to assist in the building of governmental and economic institutions and infrastructures in post-war Europe, provides training and technical assistance to find practical solutions to the legal, economic, and financial problems of developing countries and emerging economies. Since 1983, ILI has become an independent organization and is headquartered in Washington, D.C., with four international regional centers. ILI's mission "fostering prosperity through the rule of law" helps to raise the levels of professional competence and capacity in all nations so that professionals may achieve practical solutions to common problems in ways that suit their nations' needs. www.ili.org

22. Johnson Law Group International

Johnson Law Group International, through its Lawyers for International Development™ program, maintains an international development technical assistance consulting practice, particularly on issues related to governance reform. Lawyers for International Development™ provide technical expertise in the following areas: rule of law, administrative law, regulatory reform, commercial law reform, judicial reform, anti-corruption, conflict management and mitigation, alternative dispute resolution, national policy reform, and law and security. Assistance includes support in program assessment, design, and implementation; training and knowledge transfer; and performance monitoring and evaluation. www.jlgi.com

23. Management Sciences for Development, Inc. (MSD)

MSD is a woman-owned, for-profit corporation with more than 20 years of experience partnering with USAID to implement rule of law and human rights programs in fragile countries around the world. MSD provides training and technical assistance to governments and civil society to build a culture of lawfulness that respects and upholds the rule of law. MSD has expertise in justice sector reforms, victim advocacy and early-warning systems, and conflict and dispute resolution, including alternative dispute resolution and community justice programs. MSD is committed to increase access to justice for marginalized populations, including women and children, the displaced and disabled, and other minority groups. MSD implements programs across the rule of law spectrum throughout Latin America and the Caribbean, and in Africa, the Middle East, and Asia. www.msdglobal.com

24. Management Services International (MSI)

MSI, a subsidiary of Coffey International, Ltd., is a Washington, D.C.–based international development firm providing specialized short- and long-term technical assistance. Since its 1981 founding, MSI has grown in size and technical scope, implementing and managing more than 70 projects worldwide. MSI has substantively diverse and geographically broad experience in the rule of law sector. With expertise in access to justice, judicial reform, human rights, trafficking in persons, civilian policing, and institutional capacity building, MSI is involved in judicial training, legal aid networks, alternative dispute resolution, and institutional capacity-building activities in Eastern Europe, the former Soviet Union, Latin America, and the Middle East. As judicial processes are often fraught with corruption, or perceived to be, MSI incorporates transparency and ethics activities into its rule of law programming. Similarly, throughout its work, MSI integrates monitoring and evaluation in its projects to ensure that interventions are tailored to changing needs and to document the impact over time. MSI has conducted sector assessments, project evaluations, and program design for a wide range of justice projects. www.msiworldwide.com

25. Millennium Partners

Millennium Partners is a small business that has experience in anticorruption and rule of law, public administration, capital markets, civil society strengthening, education, health, women's issues, local government strengthening, media, privatization, small and medium business development, and trade and foreign investment. www.millenniumpartners.org

26. National Center for State Courts (NCSC)

NCSC, founded in 1971 at the urging of Chief Justice Warren Burger, has provided U.S. state courts with cutting-edge research, training, and consulting in court management and administration for 40 years. In the early 1990s, NCSC established its international office to provide rule of law–related consulting and assistance to non-U.S. courts and justice systems. NCSC offers a comprehensive set of resources for working with justice systems in developing and post-conflict countries. It provides expert technical assistance in court management, alternative dispute resolution, institutional capacity building of justice sector organizations, judicial independence, criminal and civil justice reform, legal and judicial reform, and expertise in diverse law systems, including civil law and common law, Shari'a law–based and traditional settlement systems. NCSC has implemented more than 70 rule of law projects in over 30 countries in the regions of Africa and the Middle East, Asia, Eastern Europe, Central Asia, Latin America, and the Caribbean. www.ncscinternational.org

27. Open Society Foundations (Open Society)

The Open Society was established by George Soros in 1984 to help countries make the transition from communism and has grown to encompass more than 70 countries in Europe, Asia, Africa, and Latin America. It works to build vibrant and tolerant democracies whose governments are accountable to their citizens. To achieve this mission, the Open Society seeks to shape public policies that ensure greater fairness in political, legal, and economic systems and safeguard fundamental rights. On a local level, the Open Society implements a range of initiatives to advance justice, education, public health, and independent media. At the same time, the Open Society builds alliances across borders and continents on issues such as corruption and freedom of information. The Open Society places a high priority on protecting and improving the lives of people in marginalized communities. www.soros.org

28. The PAE Group (PAE)

PAE's activities include police mentoring, judicial assistance, and correctional officer training. PAE is in over 30 countries, engaged in positive partnerships with host country governments and local civil institutions as well as the U.S. Department of State, U.S. Department of Defense, and international aid agencies. PAE's program management office maintains a cadre of experienced law enforcement, corrections, and justice professionals ready for assignment overseas. The PAE justice support team consists of civilian police, attorneys, judges, corrections officers, and others to assist in the establishment and maintenance of contemporary law-and-order techniques in priority areas around the globe. www.paegroup.com

29. QED Group, LLC (QED)

QED is a full-service international consulting firm that provides practical solutions to social problems through sound analysis, proven management techniques, and creative implementation. Founded on monitoring and evaluation, QED has completed rule of law assignments, including conducting assessments and evaluations, developing rule of law strategies, advising justice sector officials on best practices, supporting cooperation among government institutions, and facilitating mechanisms for public participation in legal reform and policy decision making. www.qedgroupllc.com

30. Social Impact (SI)

SI is a global social enterprise dedicated to creating dramatic improvements in the performance of organizations and programs working to enhance the social and economic well-being of people around the world. SI provides a full range of innovative management consulting, technical assistance, and training services to strengthen international development programs, organizations, and policies. SI works across sectors to promote peace and democratic governance, strengthen civil society, foster economic growth, and protect the environment. www.socialimpact.com

31. Tetra Tech DPK (Tt DPK)

Tt DPK is a San Francisco–based firm that provides technical, management, and advisory services to help developing and transitioning societies and governments navigate the challenges of modernization and democratization. Tt DPK has implemented more than 80 rule of law, governance, and civil society strengthening programs around the world for donors, including the U.S. Department of State, USAID, and multilateral banks, such as The World Bank and Asia Development Bank. Tt DPK's focus is to help establish and strengthen productive relationships between state and society and to develop government and justice systems that are responsive, transparent, accountable, fair, and efficient. Tt DPK recognizes that good governance and the rule of law are basic qualities of successful democratic societies and market economies. Tt DPK carries out its mission by: (1) helping institutions and organizations plan, manage, and implement change to provide fair and timely access to justice; (2) operate under transparent rules that safeguard rights of individuals, stimulate economic growth, and guard against unethical or corrupt practices; (3) ensure the efficient and effective delivery of services to the public; and (4) increase opportunities for citizens to participate in the political and economic decisions that affect their lives. www.tetratechdpk.com

E. Membership and Subscription Services for International Rule of Law Attorneys

In addition to contacting the technical assistance providers directly through their websites, there are several other avenues by which attorneys can find employment opportunities as well as connect to other international rule of law attorneys.

1. Devex

Devex is a membership organization delivering business information and recruiting services to the international development community. It connects aid workers and development professionals to a network of information, people, and ideas, enabling them to have more impact for more people. Devex uses web technology to deliver development business newsletters; contract, grant, and partnership opportunities; industry analysis; and recruiting services to more than 1,000 of the world's international development organizations. The Devex global platform creates market competition for projects, gives professionals from the developing world an opportunity to work on aid projects in their own countries, supports non-governmental organizations and donor agencies to attract and recruit qualified individuals, and informs a global industry. Devex is free to join. www.devex.com

2. InternationalJobs.com

InternationalJobs.com is a career portal with a worldwide audience that provides employers with immediate access to a diverse, targeted audience of job seekers looking for global employment opportunities. InternationalJobs.com attracts experienced international professionals, expatriates, and specialized job seekers and employers in a wide range of industries, including international law, international relations, international finance, management, marketing, security, global nonprofit, and human resources. www.internationaljobs.com

3. *Opportunity Knocks*

Opportunity Knocks is a national online job board and career development destination focused exclusively on the non-profit community. It also provides a resource for forms, checklists and procedures, and an annual performance kit. Opportunity Knocks is committed to leading and supporting efforts that help further non-profit careers and promote a robust workforce that enables organizations to achieve their missions. Opportunity Knocks provides a destination to find non-profit jobs and access valuable resources for developing successful careers in the non-profit community. www.opportunityknocks.org

4. *Foreign Policy Association (FPA)*

FPA was founded in 1918 and serves as a catalyst for developing awareness and understanding of, and providing informed opinions on, global issues. Through its balanced, non-partisan programs and publications, the FPA encourages citizens to participate in the foreign policy process. With over 3,000 participating employers, the FPA's Global Job Board is a source of positions for internationally minded professionals. NGO, commercial, and government opportunities around the world are posted daily and made available in a free weekly email digest. www.FPA.org

5. *International Network to Promote the Rule of Law (INPROL)*

INPROL is a global, online community of practice comprising 1,700 rule of law practitioners from 120 countries and 300 organizations. While members come from a range of disciplines and backgrounds, all have in common their work on rule of law reform in post-conflict and developing countries, either from a policy, practice, or research perspective. They share a desire to learn and innovate together as a community to improve their rule of law knowledge and practice. Membership is free and open to individuals who are currently working on rule of law and policing reform/assistance in a post-conflict or developing country in either a policy, practice, or research role. www.inprol.org

6. International Rule of Law Directory (ROL Directory)

The International Bar Association publishes the *International Rule of Law Directory*, which aims to provide users with reliable information and a compiled directory of Internet resources and links to organizations offering assistance in the rule of law. www.roldirectory.org

7. International Development Law Organization (IDLO)

IDLO publishes the *Rule of Law Assistance Directory*, a global inventory of development assistance activities in the field of legal and institutional reform, The Directory contains a global database of rule of law projects and national justice strategies. www.idlo.int/english/Resources/ROL/Pages/default.aspx

8. LinkedIn

Technical assistance providers seeking qualified candidates for rule of law positions subscribe to LinkedIn Recruiter, which gives them full access to its millions of users. As they can search by name, company, sector, and/or keyword, international rule of law attorneys seeking employment opportunities may also have a LinkedIn page with a complete description of their background and qualifications. Additionally, LinkedIn hosts a Rule of Law Veterans discussion group.

9. Facebook

Many technical assistance providers have a page on Facebook in addition to their own website, where they list their current activities and often post vacancies and immediate employment needs.

F. Rule of Law Academic Courses

There are several law schools and organizations, as well as the U.S. Department of State and the U.S. Department of Defense, that provide rule of law courses. At least one law school provides an LL.M. in the rule of law. While some of the courses listed below may not currently be given, a description of the courses is helpful to an understanding of the depth and breadth of rule of law instruction. This list is not exhaustive, as law schools continue to enhance their curriculum concerning international law and rule of law courses.

1. School of Law of Loyola University Chicago (Loyola)

Loyola offers a fully accredited, practice-oriented, one-year LL.M. program in Rule of Law for Development (Prolaw) at its Rome, Italy, campus. Prolaw is taught by experienced rule of law practitioners and is designed to equip its internationally recruited students with the practical knowledge and skills needed for rule of law advisery work in developing countries. The focus is on what rule of law advisers actually do once on the job and the knowledge and skills needed for success rather than on particular areas of law. It offers extensive networking opportunities with international development organizations and visiting practitioners from around the globe to enhance onward career development in the field. www.luc.edu/prolaw.

Loyola also offers the Rule of Law in Developing Legal Systems course at its Chicago campus, which helps students gain an understanding of the emerging field of rule of law reform by examining the design and implementation of a variety of legal and judicial reform initiatives in developing countries. Initially, the definitions of "rule of law" are examined and the class explores the clash of different objectives behind rule of law reform programs, including democracy promotion, economic development, promotion of human rights and social justice, and law enforcement. The role played by a functioning, effective, and accessible justice system in economic growth and sustainable, equitable development is examined, and programs implemented in selected developing countries as well as issues raised by overlapping or inconsistent agendas of foreign donor nations and international and regional organizations are discussed. www.luc.edu/law

2. United States Institute of Peace (USIP)

USIP periodically conducts the Rule of Law Practitioners course, drawing upon on-the-ground experience, lessons learned, and best practices. The course offers a comprehensive introduction to the rule of law from theory to practical application. Through the use of case studies and interactive exercises, participants practice core rule of law skills and examine the dilemmas faced in rule of law promotion. www.usip.org

3. University of Minnesota Law School

The Rule of Law seminar examines the concepts and core principles of the rule of law. Seminar sessions are devoted to identifying the meaning of the terms "rule of law" and "independence of the judiciary." The importance of a strong and independent legal profession to the rule of law is discussed. Seminar sessions focus on such issues as the problem of corruption and the rule of law, the relationship between human rights and the rule of law, and the challenges of war and genocide. The relationship between the rule of law and economic development and alleviation of poverty is also explored. The seminar includes a discussion of the responsibility of lawyers to support and promote the rule of law within their own country and in developing countries.

The Rule of Law seminar is taught by Robert A. Stein, who served from 1994 to 2006 as the Executive Director and Chief Operating Officer of the American Bar Association.

4. Stanford University

The Ford Dorsey Program in International Policy Studies offers several courses in democracy, development, and rule of law. The gateway course demonstrates links among the establishment of democracy, economic growth, and the rule of law. It leads to discussion of how democratic, economically developed states arise; how the rule of law can be established where it has been historically absent; how the variations in such systems function and the consequences of institutional forms and choices; and how democratic systems have arisen in different parts of the world. It provides available policy instruments used in international democracy, rule of law, and development promotion efforts. http://ips.stanford.edu/courses_concentration_democracy

5. Georgetown Law School

The Nation Building and the Rule of Law course helps students develop an understanding of the strategies and methodologies employed by international actors engaged in rule of law development and the legal and policy dilemmas implicated by such activities. The course explores what is meant by "establishing the rule of law" in the context of a post-conflict state, and examines critiques of this emerging field of practice. The course addresses the principal substantive areas in which domestic reformers and their international advisers and funders engage in rule of law building, including law reform, judicial reform, and anti-corruption and legal empowerment. www.law.georgetown.edu/curriculum

6. *American University Washington College of Law*

The Global Corruption and Rights course is largely designed to paint a global picture of an emerging global legal and governance landscape that is only now poised to unite a wide range of stakeholders, including the legal profession, around an agenda to globalize the rule of law and to reduce and prevent corruption in emerging markets and the developing world. Through case studies, students learn how to help their client fully understand and better calculate the costs and risks of working in countries where government institutions such as the judiciary are very weak or endemically corrupt and where the laws sound good on paper but are not implemented in practice.

7. *University of South Carolina*

The Rule of Law Collaborative (ROLC) organizes conferences and training workshops for U.S. government agencies, human rights organizations, and foreign scholars and officials. The ROLC also partners with other institutions, law schools, non-governmental organizations, and the World Justice Project in striving to promote justice and human rights in fragile and post-conflict zones. The ROLC draws on the expertise of more than 50 faculty associates from a broad range of disciplines who undertake research relating to rule of law, conflict resolution, and human rights promotion. www.rolc.sc.edu

8. *International Law Institute (ILI)*

Focusing on fostering prosperity through the rule of law, ILI conducts a series of training programs annually at its headquarters in Washington, D.C. The programs are geared for government officials, academics, legal, and other private-sector professionals. The training programs specialize in legal, economic, management, legislative, and governance matters, and cover such topics as arbitration and mediation, judicial administration, corporate governance, legislative drafting, project management, and negotiating and implementing trade agreements.www.ili.org

9. *University of San Francisco (USF) Law School*

In conjunction with USF Law School's Center for Law and Global Justice, which manages and participates in international rule of law programs in developing nations, the International Externship Program in Developing Nations (Program) is offered in Argentina, Cambodia, China, Haiti, India, and Vietnam. The Program provides an overview of the law and legal institutions relating to the country's most pressing rule of law issues, such as access to justice, human trafficking, children's and women's rights, and anti-corruption legislation, and provides an opportunity to complete an internship with a human rights/ rule of law non-governmental organization. USF Law School also conducts a seminar on International Development and the Rule of Law covering such rule of law issues as corruption, court reform, criminal justice, empowerment of women and children, elections and political processes, various forms of economic development, and environmental protection.

10. UC Hastings College of the Law (UC Hastings)

UC Hastings is typical of many U.S. law schools today by offering various seminars that address rule of law issues, such as the Law and Development Seminar, which focuses on international institutions, the role of law in development, the rule of law and legal empowerment, and sustainable development; the Moral Foundations of Western Law Seminar, which explores the ethical presuppositions that Western legal systems embrace the rule of law; and the Islamic Finance and Transactions Seminar, which examines the growing intersection between Sharia-related transactions and the American notion of the rule of law.

G. Rule of Law Publications

There are several excellent rule of law publications providing a theoretical perspective as well as a practical application of enhancing the rule of law, some of which are listed below.

1. World Justice Project

The World Justice Project, founded as an initiative of the American Bar Association in 2006 and established as an independent, tax-exempt, non-profit corporation in early 2009, publishes the *Rule of Law Index*® as part of its mission to lead a global, multidisciplinary effort to strengthen the rule of law for the development of communities of opportunity and equity. The *Rule of Law Index®* is a quantitative assessment tool designed to offer a detailed and comprehensive picture of the extent to which countries adhere to the rule of law. The *Rule of Law Index®* provides detailed information and original data regarding a variety of dimensions of the rule of law, which enables stakeholders to assess a nation's adherence to the rule of law in practice, identify a nation's strengths and weaknesses in comparison to other countries, and track changes over time. www.worldjusticeproject.org

2. U.S. Agency for International Development

Rule of Law Strategic Framework

A Field Guide for USAID Democracy and Governance Officers: Assistance to Civilian Law Enforcement in Developing Countries

Rebuilding the Rule of Law in Post-Conflict Environments

Reducing Corruption in the Judiciary

Guidance for Promoting Judicial Independence and Impartiality

Case Tracking & Management Guide

Achievements in Building & Maintaining the Rule of Law

Alternative Dispute Resolution Practitioners' Guide

Weighing in on the Scales of Justice

www.usaid.gov/our_work/democracy_and_governance/
technical_areas/rule_of_law/

3. U.S. Department of Defense

DOD has published the *Rule of Law Handbook—A Practitioner's Guide for Judge Advocates, 2011*, which provides a framework for conducting rule of law missions in the context of U.S. military interventions. It is, however, an excellent guide for all rule of law practitioners.

4. The World Bank

The World Bank's flagship publications that have a major rule of law component are:

World Development Reports—go.worldbank.org/LOTTGBE9I0
- *World Development Report 2012: Gender Equality and Development*
- *World Development Report 2011: Conflict, Security, and Development*
- *World Development Report 2006: Equity and Development*
- *World Development Report 2002: Building Institutions for Markets*
- *World Development Report 1997: The State in a Changing World*

Justice and Development Working Paper Series—go.worldbank.org/0ZLUNJ7RU0

World Bank Institute's Governance and Anti-Corruption Publications—go.worldbank.org/4TGCU32GX0

Justice for the Poor Program Publications—go.worldbank.org/ZRKELPETD0

5. United Nations

Approach to Assistance for Strengthening the Rule of Law at the International Level, 2011, is a guidance note of the Secretary-General of the United Nations. www.unrol.org/doc.aspx?d=3063

6. International Network to Promote the Rule of Law

The International Network to Promote the Rule of Law has recently launched its publication series, Practitioner's Guides. Each Guide is a primer on a specific rule of law issue or area. It seeks to provide an introduction and overview of this area, as well as distilling best practices and approaches, where relevant. The first Practitioner's Guide is *Common Law and Civil Law Traditions*, which provides an overview of both comon law and civil law legal traditions—comparing and contrasting them—so that practitioners deploying to post-conflict or developing countries can become familiar with them and more easily work in a country that follows an unfamiliar tradition. www.improl.org

7. International Judicial Academy

The International Judicial Academy, with assistance from the American Society of International Law, publishes the *International Judicial Monitor*, an international law resource for judiciaries, justice-sector professionals, and the global rule of law community. www.judicialmonitor.org.

H. Conclusion

International rule of law attorneys are in the enviable position of not only enhancing the capacity of legal professionals, but also of having a lasting impact on governmental and non-governmental institutions involved in legal education, legal professional services, and judicial reform. Although their income will not match that of private practitioners, the work of rule of law attorneys is priceless, as the lives of others are often changed because of the efforts of rule of law attorneys.

Part 4

Practice Tips and Methodology

Using the Internet to Develop a Small-Firm International Law Practice

12

by Jeffrey M. Aresty and Priscilla B. Pelgen[1]

As emerging technologies become more important in defining new ways of practicing law over the Internet, the legal professional will continue to be affected in a myriad of ways. For example:

- Bright young law students and lawyers alike have more chances than ever before to establish careers in solo settings practicing private international law;
- Practicing lawyers everywhere can reinvent their practices in cyberspace and deliver legal information and services through the Internet in a wide variety of methods; and
- There is a growing need for lawyers to counsel and resolve disputes online.

---

1. The authors are working together at the Institute of the Internet Bar Organization to empower a new breed of lawyers to practice, compete, and contribute to a globally connected society. The authors appreciate and acknowledge the contribution of Andrew Barnes, Jeff Aresty's former law partner, and Edward Rholl, former executive director of Internet Bar Organization, who were co-authors of prior versions of this chapter. They also appreciate the wonderful editing skills of their colleague, friend, and editor, Salli Swartz.

155

Cyber law is the most important field of legal study in our new consumer information age. The legal profession is in the process of reinventing itself online. New and exciting roles for lawyers are emerging in solo practice. Emerging technologies provide information communication and management opportunities, enabling lawyers to design new practices with the benefits of efficiency, freedom, and real work-life balance. In the international setting, growth in the use of online dispute resolution technologies is a promising new technology that will create roles for lawyer-neutrals to resolve cases across borders.

A. Working in a Global Legal Environment

1. The Impact of the Internet on the Practice of Law

Global Internet usage brings both new technologies and practice realities, and many have not figured out how to adapt and thrive using such technology. Our global information age is driving rapid changes in client service and efficiency expectations in commercial, business, family, and even wills and estate law. The Internet has thousands of websites providing legal information, legal-oriented products, and quasi-legal advice in a wide range of areas, changing the position of power between the legal profession and the clients it serves. People want to be empowered. They want to take responsibility, be proactive, and perform some of their legal work themselves. Clients routinely turn to the Internet for initial research on their legal matters before engaging the services of a lawyer.

What has changed since this chapter was written for this book's third edition is that, for the first time in history, technological advances now enable non-lawyers to compete with lawyers for a market share of legal service products. The initial effects of this new rivalry are forcing business changes within small and large law firms alike. The result is that lawyers who formerly practiced in large and small firms are transitioning into solo practice. Market competition is fierce. The winners of today are lawyers who focus on delivering a high-quality, customized experience for their clients. Clients recognize that basic legal work is created from forms and templates of relatively equal quality across competent law firms. This client realization, combined with the new non-lawyer competition, means lawyers must innovate to be competitive and remain relevant. For example, in stark contrast to lawyers, non-lawyer companies selling legal information do not have to wrestle with the economical impact of ethical rule compliance on their bottom line, except to the extent that they can be charged by regulators with the unauthorized practice of law. Companies like LegalZoom (http://legalzoom.com) are battling these cases, settling them, and continuing to do business. Eventually, a consumer who watches LegalZoom's ads will have a hard time distinguishing between the services LegalZoom offers and what a law firm offers. Even lawyers in international practice have to take notice, as the trend of non-lawyer competition has been evident in multidisciplinary practices throughout the world for some time now. Effective competition by lawyers today necessarily includes mastering innovation, technological proficiency, and entrepreneurial skills, such as efficient business management. Lawyers must learn to differentiate themselves and their services from their competitors. A legal education and licensure is not the end of career preparation any longer; it is only the beginning.

B. The Complexity of Cyber Law

Cyber law is complicated and complex: A photographer in Kansas can post her pictures to Shutter Stock (http://shutterstock.com) and sell them to a company in Hong Kong. What law will govern the sale? A jeweler in Egypt can sell his products via online catalogs at Blue Nile (http://bluenile.com). If a dispute arises, what jurisdiction will be competent? A coffee plantation in Kenya ventures with Starbucks and sells coffee in thousands of stores globally, as well as online from the Starbucks website. What governing law and jurisdictions will apply? Who will make these decisions? What lawyers and institutions will be involved?

C. New Online Services and International Rules Promoting Online Dispute Resolution

The emerging fields of online mediation and arbitration are radically changing the landscape of international dispute resolution, with significant developments occurring in 2012. First and foremost, the legal landscape is beginning to favor the emergence of an online justice system. The European Commission submitted legislative proposals empowering all EU consumers to resolve contractual disputes online, without court involvement, and regardless of product or service involved and country of purchase origin. The Commission is working toward the creation of an EU-wide, single online platform for complete contractual dispute resolution. This online alternative will enable its participants to resolve their contractual disputes, wholly online and within 30 days. In addition, UNCITRAL WG III is expected to agree upon the draft online dispute resolution (ODR) rules for cross-border, low-value, high-volume e-commerce disputes and minimum prescribed criteria for ODR providers and neutrals.

In the United Kingdom (UK) and Europe, companies like The Claim Room (http://themediationroom.com) and Juripax (http://juripax.com) are providing the online forum for companies throughout Europe to more quickly, efficiently, and directly resolve a wide range of disputes. In the United States, the vast commercial success of eBay is in no small measure due to its use of ODR tools created by Square Trade (http://squaretrade.com) and Modria (http://modria.com) that engender trust, reduce time and cost issues, and limit liability for the sellers. In addition, local courts are beginning to explore the use of Internet-based dispute resolution technology for small claims, family law, and other types of cases.

In the United Kingdom, nearly all personal injury cases must now go to mediation before any hearing in court. Money claims cases for UK plaintiffs and defendants can be made electronically, without a lawyer, using the Money Claim Online (MCOL) Internet service, provided by the government (http://moneyclaim.gov.uk). Another example is the joint venture between the American Arbitration Association and Cybersettle. Cybersettle's blind-bidding software, used as part of an online settlement process, is linked with American Arbitration Association conciliation, mediation, and arbitration.

What is truly exciting for the solo or small firm lawyer who is interested in an international practice is that the trend toward mediation and arbitration is now met by and even pushed by the emergence of these online spaces for case resolution along with rule-making efforts in the EU and at UNCITRAL. Because the greatest economies of usage fall into the realm of disputes between parties separated by hundreds or thousands of miles, the technology's promise is potentially greatest in the international realm. The solo or small-firm lawyer with international interest and skill in using online mediation and arbitration will be increasingly in demand as counsel, adviser, or neutral.

D. The New Tools of Cyber Lawyers

During the last decade, a large cottage industry has sprung up, mostly online, which provides a stunning array of legal material at much less cost than what it would cost to get such materials from a law firm. Savvy lawyers welcome this change as a huge opportunity to expand their practices well beyond the traditional billable-hour or contingency-fee agreement. The most innovative firms offer free legal information online, the ability to schedule a telephone consultation online, and a secure extranet/web space in which their clients may communicate and collaborate.

Lawyers who understand and master ICT software applications that allow them to repurpose intellectual assets as legal information products will increase market position by providing deeply needed services to large numbers of people who are currently priced out of the market. At the same time, such lawyers will increase their business clientele and the scope of work to be done for that clientele by adapting the way they deliver services to the demands for efficiency and lower pricing coming from all corners of the business world.

For the solo or small-firm international practitioner, there are several fun, engaging, and inexpensive ways to leverage technology and their own intellectual assets to create a mobile, client-centric, 24/7 law practice tailored for the networked world. First, lawyers can repurpose written materials as e-books, e-guides, and e-kits that can be sold as legal information products. Second, lawyers can create online education simply and inexpensively using tools like PowerPoint and Articulate, and then publish these courses on their own websites as educational products. Lawyers can use blogs and podcasts to communicate ideas, build brand awareness, and generate business. They can also publish podcasts, educational programs, and materials in the e-book genre on other websites catering to people seeking legal information. These legal information products can be provided free to generate client-based business, for a fee to generate non-billable-hour revenue, or in both formats for different audiences. The provision of strictly legal information products, within the bounds of ethics and good judgment, will open a window into the global marketplace, establish you as a high-quality, trusted source of useful information, and almost inevitably lead to more traditional client business.

Moreover, as more lawyer relationships are moving online, trusted communities of lawyers (http://internetbar.org) have formed to shape a fair and accessible online justice system to meet society's needs. Finally, law firms can use tools such as virtual collaboration to expand their web presence beyond simple online brochures to an interactive presence that has the power to change their practices.

E. How We Use the Internet Effectively with Foreign Clients

Our firm provides international business law services to clients located outside the United States. One client located us on the Internet through an international listing of business professionals and introduced other clients to us.

For the first client, we outlined the scope of services required via e-mail and telephone communications before entering into a fee agreement. Because the client is based in Canada and we are located in Boston, the Internet provided the best communications tool for this relationship. Because this Canadian client's service will be offered over the Internet to users around the world, there were several international legal issues in addition to U.S. laws that had to be reviewed. International treaties (intellectual property and arbitration) were examined. U.S. and Canadian securities laws were examined and reviewed, in addition to specific communication with regulators in both countries. Because the client's business was somewhat novel, we were required to interpret existing law, policy, and culture in order to provide an opinion on how regulators from different countries would react. In the absence of an applicable global legal regime, we assisted our client in developing a globally compliant operational plan for ??????.

Currently, we are exploring new technologies, such as online deal rooms and online case management centers, and examining how these online rooms will permit us to facilitate the services we provide to our clients. Giving clients secure online access to their files and the firm research materials, along with the chance to communicate with us confidentially, will become the norm in the near future. These tools will replace the inconveniences of the time and cost of telephone calls and meetings with more efficient service and information.

A client from the United Kingdom, referred to us via an e-mail from a colleague, had been selling its products in North America without a formal agreement for several years. We had an initial brief telephone conversation at the outset of the relationship. From that point forward, the only communications were via e-mail and secure online meeting space. The client explained its initial needs, which were to draft a distribution and consignment relationship, and we provided a solution. We placed the draft of the document for review in a secure online space, where our comments were made asynchronously (saving on phone bills and sleep). The client wanted its existing relationships with its authorized agents in North America to remain unchanged. Because these relationships were not typical, the final agreements had to be specific to the relationship, and rules in both the United States and the UK had to be addressed. Because the laws and customs of the UK are not always similar to those in the United States, we retained UK counsel to provide an opinion regarding UK law. We established a virtual collaboration among ourselves, UK counsel, and the client.

Another international law area worth exploring is one in international family law practice. Single and divorced parents and parents from different home countries need help navigating disputes and other issues that often accompany such situations. As more companies adapt to global competition, rather than displace their employees, they are offering relocation opportunities.

F. Our Advice on Career Preparation

Traditionally, a career in international law usually began in a large law firm in a cosmopolitan city, or in a job with the U.S. government in a trade or diplomatic role, or as legal counsel to a large multinational corporation. However, in recent years many types of small international business law firms have opened up, especially online, and provide new career opportunities. It is much easier to establish a worldwide network of professional service providers and contacts by becoming active in international associations, such as the Section of International Law of the ABA (http://www.americanbar.org/groups/international_law.html), for example, or the Internet Bar Organization (http://internetbar.org).[2]

What type of personality is right for a small, private international law practice? Today's successful solo is a self-starter who directs and self-manages his or her own career beyond law practice licensure. The increased client and efficiency demands have practically eliminated the mentoring and guidance once prevalent in law firms. It is not that experienced lawyers do not want to mentor young lawyers anymore; rather, the new competition changes have forced increased performance requirements on all lawyers, leaving no time for tasks, which do not generate an immediate return on investment. Pursuing and investing in your own self-development beyond law school is critical. New attorneys need an understanding of business operations, time management, and organization systems. Developing these skills is critical to successful law practice management because there is a huge difference between working and working productively in a way that translates to income. An illustration for your review is available at my website, My Success from Scratch (http://mysuccessfromscratch.com/champions).[3]

To be successful, today's solo attorneys must develop the ability to segment, prioritize, calculate, and manage "time to task" values efficiently. For example, lawyers can usually do any task required within a law practice, such as scheduling appointments, calendaring, conflict checking, and drafting and filing documents. However, just because the lawyer can do all of these tasks does not mean he or she should remain isolated. In fact, the lawyer's routine performance of some of these tasks will cost the firm multiple thousands of dollars in annual revenue. Your ability to develop and pair your best skills with professional support staff is one quality leading directly to profitability. A young lawyer will need to develop certain skills and acquire certain tools to be successful in this type of practice.

---

2.   The Internet Bar Organization offers educational resources and training to help you supplement your international law competencies.

3.   Priscilla Pelgen offers mentoring in the areas of law practice marketing and management for solo lawyers. You may reach her via her website, http://mysuccessfromscratch.com.

G. The Tools

You will need to become familiar with the following:

1. Tools that will help you to add efficiency, reduce redundant activity, and vastly reduce ethics and malpractice issues through rules-based online calendaring and communications functions;
2. Work spaces, including deal rooms, mediation and arbitration suites, online conferencing tools, e-learning suites, and client intranets and extranets;
3. Communications tools, including e-mail, blogs, podcasts, webcasts, global Internet telephony, Wikis, and instant messaging that help you maintain constant communication with clients, prospects, and peers without being overwhelmed;
4. Business development tools, such as automated CRM, website templates, Really Simple Syndication (RSS), Web 2.0 social and business networking sites, and primary cross-over with some of the tools listed above, including blogs, podcasts, and e-learning suites; and
5. Learning how to market yourself without running afoul of ethics rules.

H. The Skills

You will want to develop the following skills:

- *Learn about the world's cultures.* Participating in law school exchange programs is one way to establish connections that will help you develop your international law practice. Our firm hosts law clerk interns referred by Boston-area international language schools for one-month to one-year positions. These schools provide certificate and training programs to students from other nations and cultures who want to learn English. Many of these students have prior legal backgrounds or have completed law school in their home countries and are seeking practical experience with English in a professional setting. In addition to our international law clerks, we have one lawyer who is of counsel and has special skills in international law and international business consulting. We participate in and organize programs for international chambers of commerce on topics of international business law and meet people from other cultures who have moved to Boston. We attend programs at law schools with an international focus, and we have created a bar association on the Internet to connect people from every culture in an effort to build trusted online communities to support the United Nations Millennium Goals.

- *Acquire a strong and solid knowledge of many different legal areas.* Electronic commerce and the different laws that apply in different legal jurisdictions or overlap in areas related to your practice choice, such as privacy laws, global cyber law, U.S. securities and banking laws, tax laws, corporate laws, and intellectual property laws, are all essential. It is useful to be fluent in many legal topics that can have an impact on international business. An excellent way to do that is to purchase a copy of the *ABA International Lawyer's Deskbook*, which provides a good overview of the many issues that require consideration before performing services for an international client.

- *Develop interpersonal skills* to help you demonstrate that you understand your clients' legal concerns and that you can resolve them. Many of the issues involved in international transactions contain cultural and communication obstacles that a simple document cannot overcome. Clients appreciate personal attention from lawyers, and a young lawyer who is properly prepared can act as a resource for the firm. Learning how to communicate effectively with clients comes only from experience, so law school clinics are valuable places to learn. In fact, client contact can be a key to your personal growth as a lawyer. Clients come in all types and from all cultures in an international practice. Learning how to respond to each client will add value to your legal career as you continue to learn and effectively manage your time and resources to the benefit of your clients. Only by demonstrating your understanding of how your client and its counterpart will form a lasting relationship can you fully and completely become an international business or family lawyer.

I. Conclusion

Our experience of the changing nature of the legal practice and how lawyers will deliver services in the future serves to strengthen our belief that verbal and written communication, the ability to pursue self-development, the ability to understand a client's business, and the ability to harness technology tools to market and deliver legal information and services to clients in the fast, efficient, and responsive way they now demand are the key ingredients to succeeding as an international lawyer in the 21st century. Only by embracing technology and the transformation of the way that legal services are beginning to be delivered globally can you succeed in a solo, small, or midsize international law firm.

Network or Not Work: The Choice Is Yours **13**

by Mark E. Wojcik

A. Introduction

This book contains a wealth of practical information for those who are serious about making a career in international law. This chapter helps you put into practice the points you found in earlier chapters, provides a few additional tips for building a successful international career, and encourages you to develop both short-term and long-range action plans for your personal career success.

But first, a little background on me. For more than 20 years, I have taught international law and related international subjects, including international business transactions, international trade law, international human rights, international organizations, and international criminal law. I am a law professor at The John Marshall Law School in Chicago. I am also a Permanent Guest Professor at the University of Lucerne in Switzerland and an adjunct professor at the Facultad Libre de Derecho de Monterrey in Mexico. I've had the opportunity to lecture and teach in many other countries around the world. And I've had the opportunity to work for a state government (when I clerked for a judge on the Nebraska Supreme Court), the U.S.

government (when I clerked for a judge on the U.S. Court of International Trade), and a foreign government (when I worked as Court Counsel to the Supreme Court of Palau, an independent country in western Micronesia).

I have worked in private practice at a firm that specializes in customs and international trade law. And I have been quite active in the ABA Section of International Law and in other bar associations that focus on international law. Because my personal career path has been tremendously rewarding for me, I hope to share with you some practical career advice that will help you either in getting started on your international job search or in focusing your present efforts into a more effective strategy.[1]

B. A Five-Point Checklist

You may have already created a list of things to do from earlier chapters in this book. (If you haven't, take a moment now to look again at the parts you underlined or highlighted.) The list here of five suggestions is by no means an exhaustive list, and it should not replace your own personal to-do list that you created from other chapters of this book. But as you read, you will likely remember things that you should be doing to help your job search—whether you are looking for your first or fifth job.. The five points here may help you focus on an action plan that you can put into place now.

1. Look at Your Resumé with the Eyes of an Employer

If you have not yet written a resumé, make that your first task. If your current resumé is the same one that you used before you started law school, update it. If you have no idea on how to write a resumé for a legal career, consult a legal resumé writing guide. If you have a resumé that you have used in a country other than the United States and if you are looking for a job here, you should know that American resumés can be quite different from ones common in other countries. You may

---

1. If you would like to know more about my personal background and career path, see Mark E. Wojcik, *Practical Career Advice for Young International Attorneys: How to Build a Killer Resume, Network Effectively, Create Your Own Opportunities, and Live Happily Ever After,* 5 ILSA J. Int'l & Comp. L. 455 (1999).

lose out on a job simply because you haven't adapted your resumé to the American job market. Conversely, if you are seeking a job in another country, you should at least know what information is commonly contained on resumés (which are generally called curriculum vitae) in that other country.

2. Get a Resumé

If you already have a resumé, be sure it is up to date. Keep it current with your employment history, education, bar association memberships, publications, and presentations. I advise keeping a basic resumé that includes all of your information, even if it means that your resumé is several pages long. You can have more than one version of your resumé. When you apply for a particular job, you can go to that current resumé, remove information that might not be relevant for a particular job, and focus it to the specific job you are seeking. Such is the wonder of resumés on a computer—it is no longer necessary to have a one-size-fits-all resumé. You can focus your resumé to make you a better match for each particular job opportunity. Keep in mind what your employer will want to see on your resumé.

Once your resumé is finished (or nearly so), make an appointment with the Career Service Office if you are still in law school and ask them to meet with you to discuss the strengths and weaknesses of your resumé. Before you meet with the Career Service Office, you should drop off a copy of your resumé in advance so that the comments you receive are more meaningful. The services of your school's Career Service Office will still be available to you even if you have already graduated, so do not be shy about using them. If you no longer live near your alma mater, you can call them and arrange for a telephone consultation to discuss your resumé (you may also e-mail or fax your resumé to them for comments). Also, ask them about reciprocal career service arrangements that your school may have with the career service offices of other law schools near where you currently live.

When you meet with the Career Service Office, be as specific as you can about your dream job. If a listing for that job comes in later that afternoon, the person with whom you met may remember to call you first, even before they post the job for others to see. Hopefully you will receive useful advice from having the Career Service Office look at your resumé, but no two individuals will have the same experience. Many career service offices have little direct experience in helping people find international jobs. They may be confused about what the term means and may think that you are looking only for a job in another country. They may tell you (wrongly) that international law can only be practiced in large cities such as Washington, D.C. or New York or Los Angeles.

But even if your adviser in the career service office knows nothing about foreign or international job opportunities, you should still get as much basic advice as you can on your resumé. Be sure that your resumé is in the best shape possible—and the advisers in the career service office can certainly help you with that even if they don't understand how to advise you on getting an international law career. Hopefully they will help guide you along other parts of your career search as well, but you may have to educate them about the wide range of international law careers.[2]

After you meet with the professionals in the Career Service Office, repeat the exercise with trusted friends and colleagues who are working in law firms or other jobs. And don't forget to share it also with your favorite professors (and especially those who teach international law subjects). Ask them simply to look at your resumé to be sure that it is in the best shape possible. You will often be amazed at how helpful this can be. And you'll also be surprised at how willing people will be to look at your resumé.

The persons looking at your resumé could help you proofread it if you specifically ask and you think they are skilled at proofreading, which not everyone does well. I cannot tell you how many times I find typos in a resumé—even, for example, in the person's e-mail address. (How can you expect to get a job offer if the e-mail address on your resumé is wrong?) But persons who look at your resumé are more than a proofreading service, and you should ask them to look at your resumé the way that an employer would. Have them be critical and seek out specific comments on anything you should change. For example, persons looking at your resumé may offer you some tips on how to make it more professional. You might be using a personal e-mail address that suggests you are not an ideal employee (e.g., laws_school_partyguy

---

2. You may, for example, want to buy them a copy of this book as a present.

@gmail.com might raise eyebrows). Persons looking at your resumé might point out that it is not as focused as you think it is. For example, if you are looking for a career involving some aspect of international law, there should be something on your resumé to indicate that interest. You might have forgotten to list that you are a member of the American Bar Association Section of International Law, or that you are a member of a particular committee that directly covers the particular area of international law in which you want to work.

When you send your resumé to other people, you are also actively enlisting their help in your job search. They will keep an eye out for opportunities that might be right for you. Put simply, the more people who look at your resumé, the better.

3. Join Professional Associations

If your resumé is not as strong as you would like it to be, see what you can do to build it up quickly. If you are still a student, be sure that you join the International Law Society at your school. I'm amazed at how many students seeking international careers will not even take this simple step. The dues are usually nominal, if there are any at all.

At some law schools, the International Law Society may be dormant, which sometimes happens after the president and other officers graduate without electing successors. Find out what you need to do to start it up again. This advice holds true for any student organization. If you are interested in international child abduction, you should join the Law Students' Children's Law Society. If you are interested in international issues affecting the environment, you should join the Law Student's Environmental Law Society. If no law student specialized society exists directly affecting your interests, you could start a new one. For example, if you are interested in international criminal law, you could create a new International Criminal Law Society at your school.

You should join bar associations—not only the Section of International Law of the American Bar Association but also state and local bar associations that may have international committees. (If you are a law student, remember that you can join bar associations—often for free— as a student member.) Bar associations provide excellent opportunities to network. Be sure to join not only the associations, but also the specific committees that are of particular interest to you.[3] These committees are smaller groups, focused on your areas of interest.

If the bar association does have a committee of interest to you, then you should attend the next meeting and introduce yourself to the chair and vice-chair of the committee. Offer your assistance to them. They will greatly appreciate your offer and will surely get back to you (make sure you have a card for this purpose). You can offer to help organize a speaker for a future meeting, or, more ambitiously, offer to help organize a panel of speakers for a continuing legal education (CLE) program. You could offer to write or edit a newsletter for the committee. For some strange reason, no one else wants this job, even though it gives you a fantastic opportunity to promote your name and will give you high visibility within the bar association committee. Be sure that the newsletter becomes a place where committee members will post job openings if permitted by the association rules.

When you are working on programs, remember to identify topics that might be of interest to other committees or sections in the bar association. The criminal law committee, for example, may be interested in a program on recent developments in extradition. The family law committee may be interested in a program on international adoption or child kidnapping. Whatever topic you choose for a program, be sure to focus on recent developments in that area. Audience members are more likely to come if new information is discussed, rather than presenting things they can read elsewhere.

I have found my memberships in professional bar associations to be particularly rewarding, both in terms of the substantive opportunities I have been able to cultivate as well as the personal friendships I have made over the years. I have found that those individuals who are most active in bar associations are often also the happiest lawyers I have met. They have found ways of balancing their professional and personal lives.

---

3.   In the unlikely event that there is no committee of interest to you, ask the bar association leaders how you can start a new committee. Again, you may be asked to help become a leader of that new group, and you may be able to use that leadership position in helping you to find a job.

4. *Invite Prospective Employers as Speakers*

When you are the one organizing a panel or program for a student group or bar association committee, you are often the one who works with other leaders to invite the panelists. Pick speakers who are working at the places where you want to work. Law students (and many lawyers) are often surprised at the generosity of attorneys and others who will agree to speak to student groups. Some (but not all) will do it for free. For the speakers, the invitation to speak is an opportunity to contribute as well as an opportunity to promote the law firm (or other entity where they are working).

If you don't know who to ask to be a speaker, ask a professor or a bar association leader to speak on a recent international development or to give suggestions for speakers. The Career Service Office, the Alumni Office, and the bar association will also have names of potential speakers. If you want to work at the largest international law firm in town, invite a partner or senior associate from that firm to speak. Make the speaker feel important. Create a nice sign to announce the event, be sure the room is set up and ready to go, and find an audience. One way to double a potential audience is to co-sponsor your event with other groups if possible. You instantly have twice the membership base for your speaker. Be the one to greet the speaker at the door, and be sure the speaker learns your name. Gush about your speaker's accomplishments during your introduction. Have a camera to take pictures of the speaker during the talk, and later with you. Send a thank-you letter after the event, and include a copy of the photograph if you both look good. Put your names on the back of the photo and jot down the date and place of the event. Give a copy of the photo to the student newspaper or bar association newsletter and ask them to run it. Find a blog (such as the International Law Prof Blog) that will put up the picture and a note about the event. Send a copy of the newspaper or a link to the blog post to your speaker, who will enjoy the unexpected additional publicity. (Do not enclose a resumé, however; the time will come for that later.)

5. *Keep Current*

If you hope to work in international law, you must be informed about current events. You may find yourself at a party or a seminar needing to say something meaningful about the state of the world. You have to go beyond the headlines in your knowledge of what's happening around the world. You should read a newspaper with good coverage of international issues. You should also read a newspaper or news magazine from outside the United States to give you differing perspectives on issues. Learn how to get these foreign news sources off the Internet.

You cannot limit yourself to newspapers and the Internet. You must also tackle more complex readings on international developments. *Foreign Affairs* and *Foreign Policy* are two well-known journals that will give you the depth of analysis that you need to cultivate. International law journals are an obvious choice as well, including the Year-in-Review issue of *The International Lawyer* published by the ABA Section of International Law. That volume is several hundred pages that describe the most important legal events during a particular year. And don't be surprised if lawyers from the law firm or agency where you want to work are authors of the articles in that volume.

Keeping current with recent judicial decisions is also important, and you should make it a point to read advance sheets or subscribe to e-mail services that will link you to the most recent cases. For example, if you are interested in immigration law, you should be reading the immigration decisions that are rendered across the country. Learn about special research tools for immigration lawyers (such as the publication called *Interpreter Releases,* which describes important new developments in immigration law). If you are interested in customs and international trade, you should be reading the new decisions from the U.S. Court of International Trade and the trade cases from the U.S. Court of Appeals for the Federal Circuit. Keep up on legislative and administrative developments too. Keeping current will also help you identify topics and speakers for any programs you might be organizing.

6. Write Something, and Before You Publish It, Ask an Expert to Read It

You need to have a writing sample. You may as well have a writing sample that has been published somewhere. As you read articles from law journals and bar association magazines on a regular basis, you will realize that writing an article is also something that you can do. Pick a topic about which you already know something, or pick a topic about which you would like to learn something and write it up. Do not be afraid of making mistakes in what you write. Mistakes happen. Even the venerable *Black's Law Dictionary* (in a much earlier edition) stated that "to be valid . . . treatises [sic] must be approved by two-thirds of the Senate." Wouldn't Williston and Prosser be surprised to learn that their books are not valid because they were never subjected to U.S. Senate confirmation? The definition should read "treaties," of course. In reviewing student papers, I often must read about violations "of the statue [sic]," and I wonder what piece of art has been vandalized. I read about the decision of the "trail court," and wonder if it meant deciding whether to camp for the night. You must proofread your drafts carefully to avoid these errors; do not rely solely on spell check or on the skills of your editors. While you may be able to survive these errors at a later stage of your career (say, for example, after you get tenure at a law school), you cannot afford to make such mistakes when you are building your reputation.

Beyond simple proofreading, however, is the need for serious substantive analysis of what you have written. You should not hesitate to send drafts of your articles to leading authorities in the field and to ask them to look at your work before it is published. If they agree, you will have the benefit of their expertise. Remember to thank them appropriately and to credit them for their assistance. After they have reviewed your article, you can also ask them to have a look at your resumé. Your resumé may be perfect by this point, but ask them for their advice about it anyway. If you haven't landed a job by now, there may be a way to recraft your resumé or to deliver it to an appropriate hiring partner or agency.

C. Getting to Work on Getting Work

The advice in this chapter—and in this book—should help you focus your search for an international career. Decide what steps you need to take now, in the next week, and in the next year. Recognize the particular benefits of getting actively involved in bar associations and their committees. Stay involved and stay focused, and don't be afraid to ask others for help along the way.

More Perspectives on Academic International Lawyering—Internationalizing the Legal Writing Curriculum and Developing International Legal Studies Programs

14

by Diane Penneys Edelman

By the time I attended law school, I knew that I was interested in doing what I'll call "things international." I had become interested in international affairs in high school, I had majored in Near Eastern Studies at college (when it was still a fledgling field), and I was thrilled that my law school, Brooklyn Law School, offered a unique course in international law for first-year law students. Back in the early 1980s, this was rare; courses in international and comparative law were generally reserved for upper-level students. Brooklyn, however, offered an elective international law version of the required first-year legal writing course. I opted to take this course—and was hooked. And so, you might say that my *entré* into international law was via the core legal skills course: legal writing.

Now, many years later, I have taught both legal writing and substantive law. I have developed, administered, and taught in legal studies programs abroad, and have developed additional ad hoc study abroad programs for my students. In short, international law—and raising a generation of law students to become international lawyers—are central to my career. Teaching international law in legal skills courses and study abroad programs, as well as developing and administering those programs, has been incredibly rewarding, and may be just the kind of career that you will find challenging and fulfilling, too.

A. How I Got There

During my second semester of law school, while my classmates were researching and writing appellate briefs based on domestic or federal U.S. law, I was busy researching the fundamentals of international law, writing an international law "memorial" and arguing before a mock International Court of Justice. I went on to be a member of Brooklyn's Jessup Team[1] and Editor-in-Chief of the *Brooklyn Journal of International Law*, and took as many international and comparative law courses as I could fit into my schedule. I was, admittedly, obsessed with learning about international law.

During the summer before my third year of law school, I worked at an immigration law firm (another great way to practice international law), and I clerked for a federal judge following graduation. Although I wasn't exposed to international law during my clerkship, I kept my feet wet by teaching the very same international law legal writing course that I had taken at Brooklyn as an adjunct professor in Brooklyn's legal writing program.[2] I did so for three years, while working full-time first as a judicial clerk and then as a litigator at a large Wall Street firm.

After clerking and practicing law in New York and Philadelphia, I came to Villanova University School of Law to teach legal writing. During my first year here, nearly 20 years ago, my legal writing colleagues and dean approved of my proposal to offer this unique course—an international law version of our traditional Legal Analysis and Writing course—to our first-year students. We have done so ever since. Now, nearly 30 years since I first taught international law–oriented legal writing as an adjunct professor at Brooklyn, I have taught this subject to

---

1. The Philip C. Jessup International Law Moot Court Competition was founded in the late 1950s and, as of 2011, featured students from more than 500 law schools from more than 80 countries. *See* http://www.ilsa.org/jessuphome.

2. When I had taken the course, one section was taught by a full-time doctrinal professor and one was taught by a short-term legal writing professor. After I graduated, neither taught this course, so the law school hired adjuncts who were "alumni" of the international legal writing course to teach the course.

more than 500 of the 700-plus Villanova law students who have taken this course to date.

B. What I Do

Typically, first-year law students at most American law schools learn *predictive* (sometimes called objective) legal analysis and writing during their first semester of law school and *persuasive* writing during the second semester. The latter usually involves some form of motion practice or moot court experience. At Villanova, we "internationalize" the second semester legal writing course, which we have titled International Advocacy, by immersing our students in international legal issues. Instead of assigning students to brief and argue issues of domestic law, we develop and assign hypothetical problems set before the International Court of Justice that involve issues such as the law of outer space, diplomatic immunity, environmental law, trade law, international approaches to discovery, and data privacy. Students receive basic training in international legal research from a law librarian, observe a Jessup Team practice round, and complete a variety of exercises in which they identify and analyze discrete issues of international law. We find that these topics engage our students in the world beyond our borders and lead many of them to explore international legal careers.

In addition to the first-year moot court experience, there are other ways to integrate international and foreign law as a legal writing professor. For example, during the first semester of law school, when students are just getting to know how domestic federal and state courts operate, a professor can assign problems that introduce students to the significant role that international and comparative law play in our own domestic courts. Interpretation of federal statutes such as the Alien Tort Statute or the Foreign Sovereign Immunities Act, for example, may be the subject of legal analysis and writing problems, as well as state law statutes that govern whether a state court may consider issues of foreign law or enforce a contract between an American party and a party from another country. Students will be surprised by the many ways that international law or the law of other nations may affect their domestic law practice in the future, whether they practice family law, draft contracts, or engage in some other area of practice. Perhaps, then, even if some students never choose to practice international law, they will be more prepared to *recognize* how international or comparative law can affect their clients' legal interests.[3]

C. My Evolving Career

Teaching international advocacy led me to another great opportunity to be an international lawyer in academia—namely, as an administrator of international legal studies programs. After I had been teaching at Villanova Law for nearly 10 years and had become the head of the law school's Legal Writing Program, the opportunity arose for Villanova to host the regional competition for the Jessup Competition. This meant that for three days in February 2002, Villanova would host some dozen or more moot court teams and would be responsible for obtaining nearly 80 judges to evaluate written briefs and oral arguments, in addition to providing food and caring for the teams and their coaches or advisers. I took charge of coordinating the weekend competition, which was very successful, and—I believe as a direct result—I was shortly thereafter asked to set up a summer law study program in Montréal. I jumped at the chance, and for the next year, my job took on a new dimension as I mastered the intricacies of developing that summer program.

Any law school that wants to offer a program abroad wants that program to be approved by the law school accreditation body, the American Bar Association. The first step, then, in planning our Montréal program was to familiarize myself with the Criteria for Approval of Foreign Summer Programs (now called the Criteria for Approval of Foreign Summer and Intersession Programs Established by ABA-Approved Law Schools[4]) promulgated by the ABA's Section on Legal Education and Admission to the Bar. The Criteria govern all aspects of

---

3. Although not the subject of this chapter, legal research and law librarianship can also be options for the budding academic or academic-minded international lawyer. *See, e.g.,* website of the Foreign, Comparative & International Law Special Interest Section of the American Association of Law Libraries, http://www.aallnet.org/sis/fcilsis/, and the Global Information Network of the Library of Congress, http://www.glin.gov/search.action. Interested individuals may follow these links, among others, to find opportunities to teach international law in the research context, either in academia or with the government, for example.

4. The current Criteria are *available at* http://www.americanbar.org/content/dam/aba/publications/misc/legal_education/Standards/2011_2012_aba_standards_cfa_of_foreign_summer_programs.authcheckdam.pdf.

the design of a summer program: the overall program, faculty and staff eligibility and responsibilities, program administration, educational program, eligibility of students, physical facilities, announcements of cancellation/change/termination of the program, and required disclosures to prospective students. Of course, the Criteria also prescribe the procedures for ABA approval of a summer program abroad as well.

Intrinsic to setting up a summer program abroad is the preparation of an application to the ABA by October 1 of the year *preceding* the first offering of the new summer program. If the Section's Accreditation Committee approves the program, the Section assigns an individual site visitor (typically, a member of the Committee), who evaluates the program during its first year of operation. During the visit, the site visitor meets with the program director and faculty, students, and host school staff; visits classes and student housing; reviews documentation relating to the program; and prepares a report following the visit. The Accreditation Committee then considers whether to continue approval of the program, and if it does, the program is approved for the next five years, barring some failure of the sponsoring school to comply with the Criteria. Subsequent site visits and reapproval processes take place during the sixth year of the operation of a program and every seven years thereafter. As the director of a summer abroad program, I am responsible for drafting our ABA filings, including both site visit documentation and annual reports to the ABA regarding our summer program.

Developing a summer program abroad is not simply a matter of paperwork, however. Rather, this process is filled with the excitement of creation and with collaboration. Having a program abroad requires your law school to develop a relationship with a law school abroad (often called a "faculty of law") or other institution abroad that will host your program, unless you work for one of the relatively small number of American law schools that has a campus abroad. For our Montréal program, I was fortunate to learn that our partner abroad, the University of Montréal Faculty of Law (Université de Montréal, or UdeM), had approached our school with its interest in developing an ABA-approved summer program; thus, we did not have to search for a partner. My work during that first year of planning, then, involved developing relationships with administrators and faculty at UdeM, visiting the campus, and working through all of the details that would make the program a success. I developed the overall program proposal for Villanova's Curriculum Committee and shepherded that proposal, as well as the individual course proposals, through the Committee and faculty review processes.[5]

Although I was not "practicing" international law, I thoroughly enjoyed getting to know my Canadian counterparts and colleagues and developing the structure and content of our summer program, in which Villanova and UdeM professors co-taught a variety of international and comparative law courses.[6] I arranged field trips to the Canadian Parliament and to the Supreme Court of Canada, as well as to a prominent Montréal firm. I taught International Advocacy in the program as well. Developing the Montréal program gave me a new, comparative perspective on American legal education, as well as an opportunity to get to know academics, lawyers, and institutions in another country that have remained part of my lifelong network of friends and colleagues.

After two years, our law school decided to reevaluate our summer program and to jointly offer a summer program in Rome, Italy, with the University of St. Thomas School of Law (Minneapolis) (UST), a law school with a Catholic tradition like Villanova's, with a natural attraction to Rome. Setting up this program, which has been offered since 2007, presented new challenges and opportunities for me as the program administrator and again as a teacher in the summer program.[7] Although, as with our Montréal program, we were fortunate to have a location for our program-to-be at the outset, this time there would be three institutions in three different time zones working together: UST, Villanova, and our host school in Rome. This time, rather than co-

---

5. Under the ABA Criteria, part I(B), "the faculty of each of the sponsoring law school(s) must approve the academic content of the program in the same manner as the curriculum of the sponsoring school's on-campus program."

6. In fact, I "exported" my International Advocacy course to the Montréal program, modifying the course to fit the summer schedule and to include some comparison of American, Canadian, and international law.

7. For the Rome program, I developed and taught a course on International Art and Cultural Heritage Law. As with teaching legal writing or other professional activities, teaching in a program abroad can lead to other opportunities. For example, as a direct result of developing and teaching this course, I came to join the Lawyers' Committee for Cultural Heritage Preservation, www.culturalheritagelaw. org, which I now serve as president.

teaching courses, UST and Villanova would each send two professors to Rome each summer to teach an agreed-upon set of courses. The courses would have to be approved by the faculties of both law schools, so my job would now involve a different type of coordination and a different version of collaboration.[8]

I first met our host school faculty and administration in Rome when I arrived during the summer of 2007 for the start of our first summer there. Since then, I have been responsible for coordinating all aspects of international studies programs, including:

- coordination with administration and faculty of our partner and host institutions;
- development of curriculum and coordination of curriculum approval process with Villanova and UST curriculum committees and faculties;
- development of program schedule and activities, trips, and program-wide speakers;
- annual revision of program website and application;
- marketing;
- budget development and reconciliation;
- preparation of ABA submissions;
- on-site supervision; and
- evaluation of program, coordination of submission of grades, and, of course, the occasional, and thankfully rare, troubleshooting.

My involvement with developing and administering the Rome program, however, was not the end point in my development of international programs for my law school. As you will learn from becoming familiar with the ABA regulatory scheme, American law schools may offer a broad variety of programs abroad, including winter intersession programs, semester or year-long programs, and "cooperative" programs

---

8. Under Part I(D) of the Criteria, "[a] substantial portion of the academic program must relate to the socio-legal environment of the host country or have an international or comparative focus." The Rome program courses have all had an international or comparative focus and/or a relationship to the Catholic missions of Villanova and UST.

(that is, semester or year-long programs of a certain size).[9] These programs may be organized by sponsoring law schools or arranged on an ad hoc or student-initiated basis.[10]

Like many law schools nowadays, our law school wanted to offer our students additional opportunities to study abroad in addition to our summer program. I therefore familiarized myself with ABA Criteria relating to additional forms of study abroad programs, and, with the guidance of my law school administration and faculty, developed our J.D./LL.M. International Studies Program. In this program, a small number of eligible students may spend their third year of law study at a partner law school abroad (or occasionally at a non-partner school) and obtain our J.D. *plus* an LL.M. degree from the school abroad in less time than it would normally take to complete both degrees.[11] In addition, we now permit students to extern with nonprofit organizations or governmental agencies or courts abroad both during the summer and the academic year.[12] I also counsel students on post-J.D. opportunities abroad, and stay in touch with our alumni practicing law abroad, as well as with alumni of our international legal studies programs who work stateside.

Although my responsibilities administering these programs do not necessitate travel abroad, I find my work stimulating and sufficiently international in nature to keep me exposed to the actual practice of international law. I enjoy mastering the various ABA Criteria, learning about legal education and bar admission abroad, communicating with faculty and administrators and negotiating agreements with our partner schools, working on projects with university counsel, and, most important, guiding our students on an individual basis to find the perfect fit for their interests and abilities. The satisfaction of learning about a student's success in securing legal employment abroad, in helping those less privileged to finance their own businesses in settings far less advantageous than our own, and in meeting with legislators to discuss international human rights is hard to describe and incredibly rewarding to me as a legal educator.

---

9. *See generally* http://www.americanbar.org/groups/legal_education/resources/foreign_study.html.

10. *See id.*

11. *See* http://www.law.villanova.edu/internationalstudies.

12. *See* http://www.law.villanova.edu/Resources/News/October%202010/Law%20Students%20Extern%20Aboard.aspx.

D. How to Prepare

Learn all you can about international law. Take courses in international and comparative law. Join your law school's international/comparative law journal or moot court team, join the International Law Students Association,[13] become a student member of the International Section of the American Bar Association and the American Society of International Law.[14]

Study law abroad. Regardless of whether you have studied abroad as an undergraduate or in any other program, you'll find that there are many opportunities to study abroad while in law school.[15] If you can take advantage of this opportunity—and you take your studies abroad seriously—you'll find that you can develop new legal and intercultural communication skills and learn about legal practice abroad, and you can set yourself apart from your classmates with your broadened perspective. And, like some of the alumni of our JD/LLM program, you can find legal jobs abroad *directly as a result* of your studies abroad. In addition, studying law abroad will give you new perspective on *our own* legal system, making you a more skilled lawyer, whether you practice here or abroad.

E. How to Get a Job

If you're intrigued by the idea of teaching international law via a law school's legal skills program, get started by networking. Contact your legal writing professor or the director of the legal writing program at your alma mater or, if you prefer to teach in a different location, contact the directors of the legal writing programs in the geographic areas in which you would like to teach.[16] You should also explore the websites of these law schools and review their current international and com-

---

13.   *See* http://www.ilsa.org.

14.   *See* http://www.americanbar.org/groups/international_law/membership/students.html; http://www.asil.org/2011-membership-rates.cfm#Student.

15.   *See supra* notes 9 and 10.

16.   If you graduated some years ago and the legal writing faculty member(s) who taught you or ran your law school's legal writing program are no longer affiliated with your school, you can find current information on the website of the Association of Legal Writing Directors, http://www.alwd.org/membership.html.

parative law course offerings. Does the law school already have any international legal skills courses to complement its doctrinal course offerings? If not, you may want to suggest that you can teach an international legal writing course when you apply for the job. Word of mouth, however, is usually the best way to start out; use your law school and professional connections to find out where legal writing teaching opportunities exist.

Keep in mind that the most efficient way to get your foot in the door to teach international law based legal writing is to teach traditional legal writing first. Preparation for a career in teaching legal writing begins, of course, with a strong legal writing background—so, if you are still a law student, work hard to excel in this important course, in your other writing-based courses, and in law school generally, and earn the respect of your legal-writing professor, to whom you will likely want to turn for a job reference when you enter the teaching market.[17]

When you clerk or practice law following graduation, be as proactive as possible. Tell your supervisors that you are interested in assignments involving international or comparative law. Work with lawyers from abroad if you can. Be active; find out which law schools are interested in developing international programs and seek them out. You may hear of opportunities through word of mouth, or you may want to explore opportunities listed on the AALS Faculty Appointments Register.[18] You may, of course, as I did, enter legal academia through a totally different means and then find your way into international program development and administration. No matter how you enter the academy, let your interest (and, hopefully, your skills) in this area be known, and involve yourself in curricular and program development. You may find yourself at a law school with a relatively large, structured, international programs office, or you may wind up being the sole legal program administrator.

---

17.   You should also search for teaching opportunities through the employment listings of the Legal Writing Institute, http://www.lwionline.org/employment_listings.html, and the Faculty Appointments Register of the Association of American Law Schools, http://www.aals.org/services_recruitment.php. Several law schools currently offer international law–oriented legal writing courses, as well as courses specially designed for international LL.M. students and ESL (English as a Second Language) law students (information on file with author).

18.   *See supra* note 17.

After you establish yourself in the global legal skills academic community, you'll see that you can develop opportunities to teach legal skills abroad. Law professors in many other countries appreciate the depth and scope of American legal writing pedagogy, and you will learn that you can teach legal writing abroad as a Fulbright Specialist[19] or with another international organization. You can further develop your career by speaking at conferences both in the U.S. and abroad that are sponsored by some of the organizations mentioned in this chapter. In addition, you can publish articles about global skills teaching. There are many avenues to pursue. The academic legal writing world can be your oyster, with many pearls to discover.

F. How to Use Networking and Resources

Once you make the decision to teach, you will find that legal writing is a highly networked, collegial academic field. The most prominent legal writing organization, the Legal Writing Institute,[20] not only posts job openings on its websites but sponsors local, regional, national, and international conferences in which new and seasoned professors exchange teaching ideas and methods, mentor one another, and build professional relationships that are invaluable for finding jobs in this field. In addition, the Association of Legal Writing Directors[21] holds annual conferences geared toward the administration of legal writing programs. Moreover, the Legal Writing Institute maintains a variety of materials that can be used to teach legal writing to international students—yet another way to "internationalize" legal writing teaching.[22]

---

19.   *See* http://www.cies.org/Specialists/. The Fulbright Specialist program offers grants for short-term teaching abroad. As a Fulbright Specialist, I taught legal writing at the European Humanities University in Vilnius, Lithuania, in October 2009 and April 2010, and helped to organize and spoke at a seminar for professors there as well.

20.   *See* http://www.lwionline.org.

21.   *See* http://www.alwd.org.

22.   *See* http://www.lwionline.org/teaching_international_students.html. Legal writing courses for international students are common in law schools that offer legal study programs for international students. *See* http://www.americanbar.org/groups/legal_education/resources/llm-degrees_post_j_d_non_j_d/programs_by_category.html#2foreign. These programs may offer the J.D., LL.M., and/or other degrees. In recent years, the annual Global Legal Skills Conference has

As with the academic legal writing community, you will find that the community of educators interested in international legal education is broad and collegial. Get involved in the ABA Section on International Law[23] and the AALS Section on International Legal Exchange.[24] Go to meetings and conferences, learn more about your field from others, and seize leadership opportunities whenever you can. The rewards of leadership in a professional organization can be great; you will develop the skills to organize panels and programs of great interest to your colleagues, and your involvement will encourage others to consult with you to develop ideas of their own. The more broadly you extend yourself, the more you will learn, the more you will share, and the more you will grow—and the more expertise you will have to offer your law school.

G. What Are the Challenges and Benefits?

Is teaching international law through the vehicle of legal writing the same as teaching what we typically call a "substantive" or "doctrinal" course in international or comparative law? In short, no. Typically, professors who teach doctrinal courses are on the tenure track and have full faculty voting rights and a significant level of job security compared with legal writing professors (this varies from school to school). At some law schools, legal writing professors are hired on the tenure track; at others, they have varying forms of job security or may even be adjunct (part-time) professors. Although a full discussion of the politics of legal writing is beyond the scope of this chapter, you can learn about the status of legal writing professors at law schools that you would like to teach at via personal contact, examination of the schools' websites, and from information compiled by the Legal Writing Institute and Association of Legal Writing Directors.[25] Status issues

---

provided a wonderful forum for learning about teaching in the broad category of "global legal skills" and for further networking with colleagues. *See, e.g.,* the website of the 2012 Global Legal Skills Conference, http://globallegalskills.net/.

23.   *See* http://www.americanbar.org/groups/international_law.html.

24.   *See* https://memberaccess.aals.org/eWeb/dynamicpage.aspx?webcode=ChpDetai&chp_cst_key=fed6fa2e-6b22-4fd4-863d-fed4e1518ed8.

25.   *See, e.g.,* articles posted on LRW Politics & Faculty Status, http://www.alwd.org/publications/politics_facultystatus.html.

aside, one of the great benefits of teaching legal writing is that you will generally teach small class sections, in which you can get to know your students well and provide them with substantial and meaningful feedback on their assignments.[26]

A career in legal academia can also provide you with a great way to balance family and career. Law teaching offers both flexibility and a good degree of predictability; you will likely have more control over your teaching schedule, and the regularity of your assignment calendar will enable you to have a fulfilling life both within and outside of law school. So, "find what you love"[27] and teach it. Before—or after—you land your legal writing job, convince your colleagues and deans that internationalizing the legal writing curriculum at your law school will help prepare their students for law practice in the 21st century.

As an international program administrator, you may be a faculty member or a member of the law school staff, or perhaps you're a hybrid—somewhere in between. If you have teaching as well as administrative responsibilities, you'll have a bit of juggling to do, especially during the times of the year when the orderly schedule that you have set up for your classroom students and the more unpredictable needs of your international program students collide. Academic life for a "hybrid" professor/administrator can be hectic, but so can the life of an international program administrator whose responsibilities do not include teaching. As in many jobs, the responsibilities of your position may well expand to fill (or exceed) your hours in the office, regardless of whether your position is wholly administrative in nature. You may also find yourself mired in paperwork or struggling to understand a wide variety of regulations, deadlines, and the like. Moreover, in a difficult economy, considerations other than educational value may constrain the types of programs that your school may offer.

As you may suspect, however, the benefits of administering international programs at American law schools can far outweigh the complexities of doing so. Working with faculty and administrators at your school and at institutions abroad will not only benefit your school, it

---

26. An excellent resource that discusses not only class size but all aspects of teaching legal writing is a publication of the ABA Section on Legal Education and Admission to the Bar, E. EASTON, SOURCEBOOK ON LEGAL WRITING PROGRAMS (2d ed. 2006).

27. *Jobs: "Find What You Love,"* WALL ST. J. ONLINE, Oct. 6, 2011.

will also broaden your knowledge of legal education in other countries and the practice and administration of justice abroad. You may develop other professional opportunities and, once again, gain valuable perspectives on how to improve American legal education and other countries' perceptions of American lawyers. Most important, you will have another opportunity to prepare your students to be top-notch, global 21st-century lawyers.

Creative Strategies for Launching and Growing an International Law Practice

15

by Janet H. Moore

A. Introduction

Perhaps no other legal field is as vast—and as mesmerizing—as international law. Whether you pursue a career in international litigation or arbitration, international trade, cross-border business transactions, public international law, or another specialty, intellectual challenges await. As you climb the international law career ladder, refer to the tips below to propel your career forward.

B. Responding to Globalization

Since this chapter was originally published several years ago, the practice of law has become increasingly global. Even lawyers with "purely domestic" practices find themselves handling matters with direct or tangential international issues. This means that to be competitive in the global economy, lawyers must cultivate a global perspective and cross-cultural competence. Lawyers who cultivate these skills have an advantage over those who do not.

1. Take a Global View

The most effective international attorneys possess not only great legal skills but also a broad understanding of global trends in business and other relevant areas. Helping clients to anticipate and address these trends shows forethought and good lawyering.

Developing an understanding of different legal systems is also invaluable. Sometimes finding a clear answer across jurisdictions and legal systems becomes impossible; however, clients need legal guidance to evaluate their options and make a good choice.

Lawyers can heighten their value by learning to spot critical issues, especially those outside their areas of expertise. Attorneys with general international practices and lawyers working in foreign offices of American-based firms particularly need such versatility. Distinguish yourself by your ability to anticipate and steer your clients away from problems—problems that less internationally sophisticated attorneys would miss. Clients will appreciate your foresight.

2. Cultivate Cross-Cultural Competence

Effective lawyers communicate with their clients in a way that helps clients absorb the information relayed. Whether your clients are business executives or government officials, having good people skills—and cross-cultural acumen—will improve your effectiveness.

International rainmaking also requires cross-cultural competence. As discussed later in this chapter, you will need powerful and plentiful personal connections, and strong, culturally appropriate communication skills to become a rainmaker. Some lawyers that I have trained in global rainmaking techniques feel anxious about the client development process. Finding a comfortable client development style—and learning to build trust across cultures—becomes vitally important to their international rainmaking success.

You can cultivate your cross-cultural competence by interacting regularly with people from other cultures, in both your professional and personal life. When you do so, enhance your rapport by matching the other person's pitch, pace, inflection, and body language.

Before meeting a potential client or employer from another culture, research that culture's norms of business behavior. Scores of books (sometimes with amusing anecdotes, like Roger Axtell's *Gestures: The*

Do's and Taboos of Body Language Around the World) and websites publish information on cross-cultural business skills. Many employees of foreign embassies, foreign consulates, and the U.S. State Department country-specific desks are willing to share their insights over the telephone. The websites of the U.S. State Department and Central Intelligence Agency, and news outlets like the BBC, share helpful information in online country profiles.

Because so much attorney-client communication occurs via email and other technology-based methods, when you have the chance to spend time with a client in person, make it count with culturally appropriate interaction. If you don't, there are dozens of culturally and client-savvy attorneys waiting in the wings to take your place.

C. Launching an International Law Career

Most law graduates at the top of their class at stellar law schools easily break into the international law field. However, lawyers without such credentials can also succeed if they persevere—network constantly and strategically, and "brand" and market themselves appropriately. It is important to cultivate and use excellent people skills, produce impeccable work, and consider taking zigzag steps up the career ladder to gain useful experience.

1. Clarify What You Seek

As an aspiring international lawyer, you should clarify which legal area you want to pursue—whether litigation, arbitration, transactional, trade, criminal, or many of the other international specialties. Understand and make sure that you are willing to tackle the accompanying complexities, uncertainties, and demands. Knowing which area interests you most will focus your career efforts.

If possible, investigate several areas simultaneously. Informational interviews, networking, and continuing legal education classes are good ways to find out about practice specialties, which will help you narrow your job search. Consider charting the pros and cons of each specialty as you go along to evaluate your options.

Once you have clarified your interests, set yearly, monthly, and even weekly goals to propel you forward. Formulate action steps (the more specific, the better) as you gather more information. Ask a peer, colleague, or coach to help you hold yourself accountable for your progress.

Don't get discouraged if the process takes more time than you had originally envisioned. In this highly competitive job market, you may need to accept less attractive jobs in order to earn income while working toward a more satisfactory position.

Realize that you may need to make multiple career moves—some lateral and some upward—to reach your ultimate career goal. Long gone are the days when an international lawyer would make partner at a firm and stay until retirement. Nowadays, many attorneys transition between the public and private sectors or jump between various law firms and companies. Regardless, clarify your goals and values through self-assessments to ensure that any job change brings personal satisfaction.

2. *Conduct a Self-Assessment*

Highly effective lawyers—regardless of their field—communicate clearly with others. Many of these lawyers also know how to create a favorable impression when they meet other people.

The first step to creating a good impression is to figure out how others perceive you. Assessments like DiSC™, Meyers-Briggs™, and Birkman™[1] will give you objective feedback about your strengths, weaknesses, personality type, and communication style. Draw on this data to improve your people skills and help you pick a practice area that compliments your natural strengths. For example, if you are an extrovert, you would probably thrive in a heavy courtroom practice but wither in an isolated, research-based position.

Sometimes there will be cultural barriers to your ideal career path. A female former colleague of mine was determined to represent American corporate clients in the Middle East. She succeeded, but in the end found the cultural barriers too wearing.

Many, but not all, limitations can be overcome with hard work. Understand your hurdles and honestly assess whether you can overcome them.

---

1.   These assessments must be taken through a qualified provider.

3. Polish Interview Skills

As you prepare to interview, try to correct any nervous habits that you might have, like twitching or poor eye contact. Videotape yourself while giving a presentation or during a mock client interview; this can be an invaluable tool for recognizing unflattering personal habits. Honing your interview skills will also prepare you for public presentations and client interviews down the road.

Videoconference interviews have become very common, especially when employers and job candidates are geographically distant. Because the camera magnifies nervous habits and shiny or overly decorative clothing, act and dress accordingly.

4. Bolster Needed Experience

Some aspiring international lawyers need to bolster their international experience before they can break into the field. As you examine yours, think creatively about any international exposure you gained through non-legal work, such as volunteer work or domestic projects with tangential international issues. This experience will boost your credibility.

If you lack international experience, obtain some through pro bono, contract, or consulting work. Many international nonprofit organizations, such as those involved in developing countries, regularly seek volunteers and short-term employees. Non-legal jobs that develop international business acumen will also strengthen your marketability, particularly for certain consulting and in-house legal positions.

Even after you land a job, continue with charitable work to boost your practice skills. Andrew Ballheimer, co-head of Allen & Overy's Global Corporate Practice, noted that continued charitable work as a trustee for Moorefields Eye Charity helped him to develop a broad range of business skills that benefited him in his legal work. Mr. Ballheimer explained that financial discipline, people management, and leadership are essential qualities for success in both roles. In addition, he found that his role as a trustee was a good way to network and develop relationships away from the usual working environment.[2]

---

2. "In Our Words," by Andrew Ballheimer, Partner, Allen & Overy, Feb. 27, 2012, *formerly available at* www.AllenOvery.com.

5. Network Vigorously

Whether you are an experienced international practitioner or a foreign LLM student searching for your first job, regular and effective networking will galvanize your career success. While job hunting, contact distant connections as well as close ones. Contacting "weak ties" has been linked to job search success because these remote connections will know of job opportunities not familiar to close friends and family.[3]

Make as many meaningful connections as you can with other lawyers in the field. Interacting regularly with experienced international lawyers will build your network of contacts and deepen your understanding of the practice area. You may even get helpful hints about choosing competent foreign counsel and other practical advice.

Mingle with international lawyers at the continuing legal education classes and meetings sponsored by the international sections of local bar associations. The Section of International Law of the American Bar Association is known for its cutting-edge programs and open and welcoming networking opportunities. Or, sample some of the programs offered by the many bar associations that focus on particular regions, such as the Inter-Pacific Bar Association.[4] Becoming involved with such organizations will multiply your network of international contacts. However, to get the best results, you will need to volunteer your time in a meaningful way, not just attend the group's annual conferences.

6. Research Culture of Potential Employers

Each place of employment has an internal culture. Try to learn as much as you can about this culture in advance by talking to former and current employees and reading information on the Internet. Make sure that you would feel comfortable working within the employer's culture.

One of my clients left his large international firm when he realized that its offices were too combative—and that the firm's culture not only tolerated but promoted this atmosphere. Another client found that

---

3. Mark Granovetter, *The Strength of Weak Ties: A Network Theory Revisited*, SOCIOLOGY THEORY, Vol. 1 (1983).

4. The Hieros Gamos website (www.hg.org) lists many internationally focused bar associations.

her international trade organization rarely promoted employees from within, stifling her career climb. In both of these cases, advance research might have uncovered these problems.

Conversely, sometimes lawyers discover a potential employer with an ideal culture. One of my clients happily left her comfortable but staid job upon finding a multinational corporation that encouraged its attorneys' autonomy and creativity.

A job that matches your values and lets you utilize your natural talents can bring real career satisfaction. Of course, you should also assess each prospective employer's international strategy.

Studies show that people feel comfortable with others who are like themselves, so you want to "fit in" as much as possible during each interview. For example, if you are interviewing with an international high-tech company, casually mention some relevant industry terminology that you have gleaned from trade publications. Or, if you are interviewing for a job with a particular legal specialty, become conversant in the fundamental concepts, jargon, and acronyms of that specialty.

Try to use idioms common to the potential employer's parlance; for example, if you are an Argentine lawyer interviewing with a Mexican employer, incorporate some of the colloquialisms of Mexican Spanish. If you are not a native speaker of the language in which you are interviewing, polish your written and spoken language skills ahead of time.

7. Seek International Work Wherever You Land—and Do It Well

Thanks to globalization, many domestic law jobs now include tangential international work. Constantly seek out projects with international aspects. For example, if you have a family law or probate practice, look for projects involving foreign parties or assets. In litigation, take on cases involving issues of foreign law, or evidence, experts, or witnesses located abroad. Working on cross-border issues will build your international expertise, confidence, and contacts. Be sure to develop strong relationships with foreign counsel whenever possible; refer legal matters to them, and they may become good referral sources in return.

Of course, once you get a cross-border project, you must produce excellent work product. Work hard and let your talent shine. Lawyers' reputations follow them throughout their careers, so do the best that you can on every assignment—whether international or not.

Ask for what you want. Whether you desire more international work, mentorship by a senior international lawyer, increased job responsibility, or business from a prospective client, ask for what you want. Do not expect others to read your mind.

Be sure to request performance feedback from clients and employers throughout your career. Although momentarily painful, negative feedback will enable you to improve. Conversely, when you get positive feedback from a client or boss, ask for a letter of recommendation. Legal recruiters report that too many job candidates lack letters of recommendation and have difficulty getting them after the fact.

D. Climbing the Career Ladder

Once you have launched your career, continue to look ahead. Whether you aspire to a promotion or a new job, keep your goals in mind.

1. Develop Portable Business

Nowadays, a lawyer's success and longevity at a law firm hinge on individual rainmaking. Law firm practitioners, whether junior or senior, should take immediate steps to develop their pipeline of business—even if doing so does not come instinctively.

If you hesitate to develop clients, identify and grapple with your barriers to rainmaking. (I've heard lawyers exclaim, "I hate client development!") However, even lawyers who struggle with introversion or shyness can find comfortable client development strategies; rainmaking may never come easily, but it does become easier with customized strategies.

One key to rainmaking success is to develop techniques suited to your individual strengths. For example, I worked with one introverted international lawyer who abhorred mingling at large gatherings. We worked on strategies for connecting with people one-on-one at those events, making them less intimidating. In another case, a very gregarious client needed to modify his networking style so that he made fewer—but more meaningful—connections. Yet another international attorney worked to implement a marketing plan from the ground up; as a recent partner, she found herself cast adrift by her fellow partners, left to fend for herself without clients or rainmaking experience. All of these attorneys discovered that by choosing rainmaking activities in sync with their personal styles and strengths, they were able to follow through with client development consistently and successfully.

Any client development effort should (really, must) begin with an ideal client profile. Define your ideal clients, and then prepare a client development plan to reach them. Too often lawyers say, "My ideal client is any client who pays my bills on time!" That's not really the case. Some clients pay their bills readily, but they are difficult to service. For example, some difficult clients may be too demanding, require too much handholding or consistently set unreasonable deadlines. Or, perhaps their work is less than ideal for any one of a number of reasons—e.g., the matters don't justify the fees that you must charge to cover your costs.

To develop a clear understanding of your "ideal client," examine your best clients and try to articulate what made them ideal. Look for characteristics that these clients (and their assignments) have in common. For example, did you most enjoy the kind, quality, or regularity of the work, or the rapport that you developed with the client? Did the work fall within a particularly interesting area of the law? One group of partners went through this exercise and discovered that they most enjoyed working with a particular kind of software client. This insight helped them to focus their future branding and marketing strategy.

Once you have a clear idea of your ideal clients, attend events that appeal to them. For example, many trade groups (such as those in the energy industry) and internationally focused nonprofits, like chapters of the World Affairs Council, put on events that attract international executives. Participating in these kinds of events will expose you to both potential clients and referral sources.

Lawyers who work globally know that a close personal relationship must, more often than not, precede a substantial business relationship. Given that developing close personal relationships is more difficult in many other cultures, cultivating certain foreign clients will take longer than cultivating American ones.

Before interacting with potential clients, polish your cross-cultural skills. Show interest in your client's culture by learning some basic pleasantries in the client's native tongue. Many American lawyers' extremely direct communication style makes clients from other cultures uncomfortable. Moreover, these clients may be far too polite to mention the offense—but they may never call again.

Personal introductions and recommendations matter a great deal in many cultures. Lawyers who aspire to international rainmaking should ask their contacts to make introductions on their behalf, and then follow up in a culturally sensitive manner.

Just as you would research the culture of a potential employer (as discussed above), research the culture of potential clients and their industries. Find out as much as possible about everyone with whom you will meet—their experience, schooling, interests, and the like. Figure out any natural connections between you that might create rapport. Customize your firm's marketing materials and adapt your pitch to the client's unique needs and culture.

Even governmental and in-house attorneys should cultivate their rainmaking savvy. This skill will be critical if they transition to private practice. Knowing how to satisfy clients certainly helps any lawyer succeed, whether in a government, nonprofit, law firm, in-house or academic practice.

2. *Brand and Market Yourself Effectively*

Your "personal brand" (or reputation) is what comes to mind when others think of you. If you do not know what your brand is, solicit input. Email 10–30 colleagues, peers, and clients and ask them to respond with 5–10 words or phrases—both positive and negative—that describe you. You will probably find that many of the comments are similar, and these reflect the strongest part of your brand.

Through this exercise, one of my Type A clients unhappily discovered that others labeled her as "tardy." In her zeal to please, she had taken to promising speedy turnarounds—and then slightly missing her deadlines. Unfortunately, this tarnished her brand. She used the invaluable feedback to improve her timeliness and reputation.

Lawyers can also enhance their public images by consciously and authentically showcasing their expertise in the media. According to Frank Sommerfield, president of Sommerfield Communications, Inc., a public relations firm that assists professionals with thought leadership, "Talking about your qualifications and track record isn't the best way to stand out from the fray in this information-jammed environment. You're better served showing your smarts and expertise by articulating the issues and challenges that your clients and constituents face—and suggesting solutions. Speaking out with an authoritative, empathetic voice can help you get more than your fair share of attention."[5]

Although every attorney must carefully comply with applicable state bar rules, law firm brochures and other marketing materials can explain international expertise. Some lawyers brand themselves as experts through traditional means, like writing articles or giving speeches. Increasingly, however, lawyers are turning to social media to share their knowledge (and enhance their brand). Countless lawyers share their wisdom through blogs and podcasts. For example, Dan Harris of Harris & Moure, pllc has grown his practice substantially through his award-winning China Law Blog (www.chinalawblog.com). Dan Harris explains, "Our blog has had such an impact on our brand that it is not uncommon for people to refer to us as 'the China Law Blog law firm.'"[6] Blogging about a wide variety of Chinese business and other topics has branded him as a China law expert. As a result, the national media seeks him out for quotes on China-related topics.

Examine your brand as it appears on the Internet. Constantly tweak your professional profiles on your law firm's website, LinkedIn, and other sites that feature you. Whenever you comment on a legal website like AVVO[7]—or any other professional site, for that matter—make sure that your comments reinforce your brand as an excellent international lawyer. Of course, ensure that any of your non-professional posts on Facebook, YouTube, Twitter, Pinterist, and the like don't detract from this brand.

E. Conclusion

The spread of globalization creates tremendous opportunities for lawyers with international experience and interest. In return, lawyers joining this practice can look forward to years of intellectual challenge, endless variety, and deep satisfaction.

---

5.   Email to Janet H. Moore dated April 27, 2012.
6.   Email to author dated May 4, 2012.
7.   AVVO.com allows lawyers to show their expertise by responding to questions from the public. The site also rates lawyers based on a number of listed factors.

Start Now: Leveraging Law School for a Global Career 16

by Dr. Isabella D. Bunn

Many readers of this guide are intent on finishing their legal education, then launching into a successful career as an international lawyer. Here are two words of advice: start now. Within reach are hundreds of ways to leverage the law school experience for a global career. Keep in mind the multiple advantages of each effort: you build substantive knowledge, make valuable contacts, discover potential opportunities, and signal your international commitment to prospective employers. In developing a strategy, consider the following checklist.

A. Focus on the Number-One Key to Success for an International Lawyer

When I make this point to law students, everyone seems to lean forward in anticipation. Perhaps they hope it entails a willingness to travel to exotic locations—in some luxury and at someone else's expense. But the key to success as an international lawyer is far more fundamental: be a great lawyer. There is no substitute for skills in research, analysis, writing, advocacy, and negotiation. There is no supplanting a thorough knowledge of civil and criminal procedure, constitutional law, tort law, contract law, and other subjects. Expertise in a global context builds on this set of skills and knowledge, then moves to another level of complexity in dealing with multiple jurisdictions or in addressing questions of international and comparative law.

B. Internationalize Your Law School Program

Some law schools are renowned for international opportunities; others may seem more provincial. But wherever you are based, it is up to you to take the initiative in internationalizing your law school program. Here are a few ideas:

- Enroll in classes with an international focus—public international law, comparative law, international organizations, international business transactions, international litigation and dispute settlement, human rights law, international environmental law, and many others.
- Join the school's international law society. If your school does not have one, start one. The Chicago-based International Law Students Association provides useful information (www.ilsa.org).
- Participate in international moot court competitions, such as the Jessup International Law Moot Court Competition and the Vis International Commercial Arbitration Moot.
- Apply for an internship or law clerkship with an international focus.
- Get involved in global initiatives, such as a specialized international law journal or a cross-border research project.
- Register to study abroad; if your school does not administer its own summer study abroad program, it may have cooperative arrangements with other institutions. You gain academic credits, a chance to learn from distinguished professors, and overseas living experience. The choice of locations literally spans five continents.
- Explore opportunities throughout the wider university. International offerings might be found in other departments or col-

leges on campus, such as political science, public policy, or business management.

C. Enhance Your International Law Credentials

There are dozens of ways to build your international law credentials, again leveraging the law school experience and moving beyond it.

- *Strive for overall academic excellence.* While international embellishments are a big plus, the fact remains that you should aim for the best possible results across the board. At the entry level to the legal profession, importance is attached to a strong grade-point average, an honors distinction, an editorial role on a law journal, an invitation to a legal fraternity, or a letter of recommendation from a leading professor.
- *Get published.* At some point in the law school program, students have the chance to undertake a research project. Choose your topic carefully, and plan to develop the project further into an article or case note. There are many opportunities for publication in traditional law journals, on-line journals, professional newsletters, and other media. This can help establish your international credentials, especially when your work gets cited on search engines.
- *Maximize your interdisciplinary expertise.* A survey of career options in the field of international law confirms the importance of linkages between subject areas. Can you set yourself apart through complementary studies or career experience? Addressing legal issues often demands an understanding of a particular industry or sector. Think of categories as diverse as cyberspace, national security, biodiversity, emerging technologies, international finance, cultural artifacts, epidemics, business entrepreneurship, and tax policy. If you need any more encouragement, check the starting-salary statistics for patent attorneys compared with their single-focus law only counterparts.
- *Pursue a graduate degree.* This may be a way to enhance your interdisciplinary expertise as noted above. It may also help dis-

tinguish your record from those of other applicants for a particular post. Do your research as to whether the substantial commitment in terms of time, finances, and opportunity costs are worthwhile. For some jobs, the need for a further diploma is not compelling. For others, such as teaching in a law school, a Master of Laws (LLM) or even a doctorate in the field may prove vital. Investigate the prospects for arranging a dual-degree program at your university, saving both time and tuition fees. With careful planning and allocation of credit hours, you may be able to attain a Master of Arts (MA), Master of Business Administration (MBA), or other diploma in conjunction with your law degree.

- *Apply for a fellowship.* A promising way to fill a gap between law school and a legal job may be to spend a year in a fellowship or paid internship. These are offered by various international organizations, civil society groups, research institutes, and foundations. Much like the law school experience, keep in mind the potential for career leverage.

- *Master a foreign language.* Depending on both the choice of language and your level of proficiency, this can open doors to legal assignments. Even some basic knowledge may help in promoting cultural awareness and building relationships with foreign counterparts.

- *Serve the public interest.* Alongside efforts to launch a legal career, consider various volunteer and pro bono opportunities. These can provide valuable experience while making a genuine contribution to many causes—from protecting civil liberties to preserving the environment to providing victim assistance.

- *Improve your legal and leadership skills.* Even opportunities that are not expressly international can provide substantial benefits to a global career. Focus on how legal and leadership skills in various contexts—whether in arguing a negligence case or serving on a local charity board—can translate into an international advantage.

- *Maintain global awareness.* You must keep up to date with global developments, watching news reports and reading sources such as *The Wall Street Journal, The Economist,* and the *Financial Times*. This is not just to shine in cocktail-party conversations. As an international lawyer, you will be called upon to advise on how emerging events may impact client interests. A revolution in the Middle East? The imposition of economic sanctions against an oppressive regime? A disruption in air travel due to a volcano? A sovereign debt crisis in the Eurozone? A swift response to legal ramifications and risk management is often essential. Global awareness will also help you develop a proactive strategy for your clients to take advantage of new opportunities.

- *Pass the bar exam.* Yes, international aspirations can sometimes tempt you away from securing a license to practice law. When I took the California bar review course many years ago, the lead instructor would repeatedly chant, "You've *got* to get your ticket!" And you do. Bear in mind that sitting for the bar exam, as difficult as that is, will never be easier than immediately after law school. Also consider reciprocity with other jurisdictions—especially with international centers, such as Washington and New York. You never know where your global career may take you, and bar membership may well be an indispensable requirement.

D.   Professionalize Your Career Search

The field of international law is highly competitive. You will need to be creative, tenacious, flexible, and willing to take some risks. By professionalizing your career search, you will maximize the chances of being at the right place at the right time—with the legal background to meet emerging needs.

Take advantage of your law school's career placement office. It is unlikely that the perfect international job offer will be handed to you in an engraved envelope as you arrive. But take the time to explore the various resources and services it provides, and be open to considering various options. You could learn how to analyze job descriptions, use online databases and social media, draft a persuasive résumé and cover letter, prepare for job interviews, or apply for fellowships. You might be introduced to alumni who can help with informational interviews. Your attention might be drawn to a position or location you had never before considered.

As the other contributions in this book make clear, widen your horizons beyond the traditional law-firm job. Consider a role as corporate counsel. Explore opportunities within international organizations, non-governmental organizations, international financial institutions, international courts and tribunals, global think-tanks, peace and development agencies. Various government departments, including the diplomatic service, also recruit international lawyers. The academic sector offers posts in teaching, research and librarianship—and global legal education is a growing specialization.

Finally, protect your brand. I gleaned this advice from a top executive in the world's leading professional networking company. Social media can be a great source of contacts in the job hunt. But they can also be tapped into by prospective employers. Even as a student, you need to ensure that your online presence enhances, rather than detracts from, your career standing. In this context, it should be recalled that much of the legal profession remains rather conservative and reputation-driven.

E. Join International Law Organizations

There are countless reasons to join international law organizations. As suggested in the introduction, this is a superb means of building substantive knowledge, making valuable contacts, and discovering potential opportunities. Participation can be through meetings and conferences, committee gatherings, and online seminars. Many such organizations have outreach initiatives for law students, providing special programs and reduced fees. Their websites offer resources on career development, including international internships and job openings. Overall, you will create a new professional network that can prove invaluable not only in the search for a position, but also in your continuing education and the performance of your responsibilities.

Here are some leading international law organizations:

- American Bar Association, Section of International Law
  Washington, D.C.
  www.americanbar.org/intlaw/

- American Society of International Law
  Washington, D.C.
  www.asil.org

- British Institute of International & Comparative Law
  London, England
  www.biicl.org

- European Society of International Law
  Florence, Italy
  www.esil-sedi.org

- International Association of Young Lawyers (AIJA)
  Brussels, Belgium
  www.aija.org

- International Bar Association
  London, England (check for national chapters)
  www.ibanet.org

- International Law Association
  London, England (check for national chapters)
  www.ila-hq.org

- Society for International Economic Law
  www.sielnet.org

- Union Internationale des Avocats
  Paris, France
  www.uianet.org

In addition, note that U.S. state bar associations and foreign national law societies often have committees that focus on international law. These can be excellent sources of local contacts.

F. Be Mindful of the Greater Good

International lawyers enjoy a measure of power arising from their expertise and the arenas in which they work. With such power comes a unique set of responsibilities. Our advice and advocacy may influence laws, treaties, government strategies, business plans, economic programs, and policy priorities on a global scale. We may be instrumental in settling disputes and resolving conflicts. Beyond the ethical principles guiding the legal profession, it is worth reflecting on our broader moral legacy. The field of international law is closely tied to questions of justice and social order; of human dignity, equality, and freedom; of humanitarian assistance; of environmental protection and sustainable development; of peace and security. The next generation of international lawyers, mindful of the greater good, can help forge a new global agenda to meet these challenges. (Yes, this means you.)

G. Stay Encouraged

The practice of international law is an exceptionally rewarding profession. Making that vision a reality can at times seem distant and difficult. But make a start by leveraging your law school experience for a global career. Find encouragement where you can, including in the words of German philosopher and poet Johann Von Goethe:

> "Whatever you can do or dream you can, begin it.
> Boldness has genius, power and magic in it. Begin it now."

One Non-linear Career in International Law

17

by Homer E. Moyer, Jr.

Being asked to reflect on one's own career may be flattering, but it is also a bit daunting. It brings to mind a worrisome comment that a friend passed on to me not long ago: "Some of the things I remember best never actually happened." Although I won't make that my disclaimer, I am nonetheless mindful that past successes are sometimes more readily recalled than frustrations, which we all encounter. Understanding that, I am happy to venture a few subjective observations—in hindsight—about an unplanned career in international law.

My career path should give heart to any lawyers who worry that they were not properly prepared for the paths on which they find themselves. A career in international law is something for which I was, in virtually all respects, unprepared. Like most of my college classmates—and unlike my children—I never had a semester abroad. Of the 30 classmates in my section of the law school dorm, I quickly learned that I was the only one never to have traveled abroad. At law school, I never took a course in international law. I had no foreign language skills, only unhelpful remnants of Spanish vocabulary.

I was plainly above average in international illiteracy. But our profession also had some way to go at that time.

The international law courses offered in law school tended to be on public international law only. There were no courses on international trade or the General Agreement on Tariffs and Trade (GATT), and those curious classmates who were interested in a career in international law had relatively few job opportunities. With one or two exceptions, there were no multinational law firms with offices in multiple countries. The State Department's Legal Adviser's Office and one or two public financial institutions interviewed at our law school, and a few large New York and Washington firms did exotic-sounding international work. Otherwise, international law was not a well-trodden career path. Rather, the common paths were those you might expect: clerkships; large firms with strong corporate, litigation, or regulatory practices; and—as this was during the Vietnam War—many opportunities for military service.

My own path led through the Navy Judge Advocate General (JAG) school (and its excellent, no-frills litigation skills training, which was then a rarity in law schools), an 18-month stint with a public interest organization that had an interest in supporting a treatise/casebook on military law, and three invaluable years at Covington & Burling, where that firm's standards of excellence were forever inculcated in my professional DNA. All of those stops were in Washington, D.C., and were thus landlocked (moderately embarrassing for a Naval officer) and entirely domestic. Each was a wonderful experience, but none pointed to a career in international law.

There was no foreseeing then that someday I might chair the Section of International Law of the ABA, an entity that was undoubtedly unknown to me at the time. My career swerve into international law came when, thanks to my friend and classmate J. T. Smith, and his extraordinary mentor, Secretary Eliot Richardson, I was invited to join them at the Department of Commerce. I recall that the White House personnel office and I both initially balked at the idea, but J.T. and Eliot persevered. As a result, I had a uniquely rich government experience and, ultimately, a clear change of direction in my legal career.

One milestone came barely a year later when, following quick enactment of the Anti-Boycott law during the early months of the Carter Administration, a new deputy assistant secretary and I were locked in a room for weeks and charged with producing implementing regulations. Out of that crucible came perhaps my first lessons in the law and politics of U.S. regulatory regimes affecting international trade and business. Other events beyond my control that advanced my international awareness while at Commerce included passage of the Foreign Corrupt Practices Act, the imposition of sanctions in response to the Iranian hostage crisis, the U.S. embargo of the Olympics, and initial trade negotiations with China. When I left the government late at night on January 19, 1981, I left with the odd notion of wanting to start an international practice, maybe one that would bring together elements of international work that, up until that time, had tended to be in separate firms or, at best, in separate, unconnected parts of the same large firm.

In reflecting on having migrated from that point in time—early 1981—to finding myself in 2012 as a senior partner in the extraordinary law firm of Miller & Chevalier, I can perhaps offer a few observations. One is that it would make good sense for anyone interested in international law to do many of the things I did not do. Spending time abroad, seeing the United States from the outside in, learning foreign languages, studying international law, finding out about civil-law systems and Sharia courts, being a conspicuous minority in a culture different from your own—all these are valuable experiences for anyone whose future legal practice is likely to involve clients, laws, and legal problems that span more than one culture.

It is undoubtedly also helpful to be prepared to be professionally nimble. None of the areas of the law on which I now focus my practice and through which I earn a living was a subject that was taught when I was in law school. Most didn't exist at all, or at least not in a recognizably similar form. For anyone who is reading this piece without the aid of reading glasses, the pace of substantive change in legal specialties in the future is likely to be even faster than it was for me. (This reality also reinforces my abiding bias that law school is really about learning to think, analyze, write, and advocate, and not about substantive learning.)

Another comforting proposition, particularly in the face of not knowing what your legal specialty may be in a few years, is that there is some value in becoming expert in small things. Glacial professional forces are putting a premium on specialization. What they also enable, however, is the likes of any of us to learn quite a lot about—and become relatively expert in—particular small topics. For example, knowing everything there is to know about "reportable requests" under the

Commerce Department's anti-boycott law may not be a universally prized asset, but it may well be of intense interest to certain paying clients and will add an identifiable badge to one's professional profile.

Small opportunities can also lead in unexpected directions. My unintended entry into the world of the American Bar Association could be traced to a request in the early 1980s that I prepare a draft report and resolution for the International Section on the extraterritorial application of U.S. export controls laws. This was a subject about which I had not yet forgotten what I had learned in government and on which I could easily gather a few others who knew quite a lot. Over two or three brown-bag lunches, we prepared a draft and then watched it bob along through the various channels of the ABA's bureaucracy until it actually was approved as formal ABA policy by a large sea of faces that I later came to know as the ABA House of Delegates. This small project, possibly together with low expectations that we would ever produce a draft, was my first step onto the slippery slope of participation in the ABA.

Through the ABA, I have come to appreciate that bar associations can be congenial venues for professional and educational experiments. One small but enduring example in my career dates from the mid-1980s when, as a new ABA trade committee desperately seeking to make our way, one of us thought that we might call an early breakfast program "Breakfast at the Bar," a format that stuck and continues to this day. Likewise, the "Practitioners' Workshop"—so labeled, as I recall, primarily because we didn't intend to serve breakfast—has survived. And the ever-successful John Jackson mini-course on the World Trade Organization (WTO)—then on the GATT—that we first offered at the Wye Plantation at about the same time continued to be one of the CLE jewels of the Section for many years. I believe that it was the first of these that attracted Jonathan Fried, later to become Canada's Ambassador to Japan, and Grant Aldonas, later to become Under Secretary of Commerce for International Trade, among others. But then again, with John Jackson as the impresario, how could those seminars have been anything other than highly successful?

Uncertain projects can also sometimes lead far beyond their original horizons. I was fortunate in the late 1980s to be able to collaborate with Sandy D'Alemberte, an indefatigable, effervescent source of innovative ideas, both as ABA president and otherwise. He encouraged and guided my improbable idea of a large, bilateral conference of American and Soviet lawyers in the then-still-communist Soviet Union. The idea got traction, and the unlikely result was the 1990 Moscow Conference, attended by over 2,000 American and Soviet lawyers and judges who met in the Kremlin to discuss 32 topics, some provocative ones of which had never before been publicly addressed in the Soviet Union. The negotiated conference schedule included a morning break to allow attendees to attend Rosh Hashanah services (a radical notion in the Soviet Union in 1990), an impromptu 30-minute soliloquy by a beleaguered Mikhail Gorbachev, and a final banquet above the massive Palace of Congresses, complete with a blues singer from New Orleans and dancing, both of which were firsts for that building.

The Moscow Conference, which commands only a modest note in the Section's archives, gave impetus, in turn, to the idea of the Central and East European Law Initiative (CEELI), launched by the Section following the fall of the Berlin Wall. Born despite deep skepticism by both the U.S. State Department and the Board of Governors of the ABA, that uncertain project survived and ultimately flourished, eventually becoming the ABA's global Rule of Law Initiative. Like so many projects that ultimately do well, CEELI's success can be explained only by our good fortune in enlisting talented, dedicated volunteers. Among CEELI's pantheon of heroes: Mark Ellis, CEELI's first executive director, who masterfully guided its growth; Justice Sandra Day O'Connor, who has become a global leader for the rule of law; the beloved and sagacious Ambassador Max Kampelman; Judge Pat Wald, who must have traveled to the region 20 or more times; Abner Mikva, whose experience and insights span all three branches of government; and many others. They, in turn, helped inspire more than 5,000 lawyers and judges who gave freely of their time to help advance the law-reform process in emerging democracies.

There are many examples of the extraordinary opportunities that pro bono work can offer in terms of professional development, satisfaction, and making a difference. Pro bono work afforded me my first civilian jury trial, a Mississippi voting rights case; a Supreme Court argument; and a front-row seat for the historic transition of more than 25 former communist countries. Firms like Miller & Chevalier that support pro bono efforts deserve more credit than they get (my CEELI hours probably totaled between four and five work years), even when some of those hours come on top of billable work. Working with CEELI—some unpaid volunteers served three or four years in the field—profoundly affected the careers and priorities of scores of lawyers and judges, many of whom point to their experiences in the field as the most rewarding of their professional lives. That this pro bono work so enriched the lives of the volunteers was an unintended but magnificent side effect of the historic work that those volunteers did.

Both the Moscow Conference and CEELI hold multiple lessons: that the potential rewards of taking occasional risks (both institutional and individual) can be substantial; that small ideas and opportunities often lead down unpredictable paths; that collaborating with smart, dedicated, visionary colleagues can be a key to success; that serving the public good remains a powerful impulse among American lawyers; and that the rule of law (a phrase that, as Justice Kennedy points out, our generation never heard mentioned in law school) is vitally important in parts of the world where it remains an unrealized ideal, not a slogan or something we take for granted. It is also enlightening and humbling to gain an appreciation of the immense challenges faced by some of our professional colleagues elsewhere in the world.

Lest this piece become more avuncular than intended, it may be appropriate to take a moment also to applaud the importance of periodic silliness and irreverence, and the laughter they engender. All my favorite lawyers have had a ready laugh. If one happens to spend extended time in Washington, irreverence should begin to come naturally—and remind us of how far we have to go in being high-minded and public-spirited in tending to the public's business. Silliness is more personal—but not without its own risks.

At a black-tie dinner of Covington & Burling lawyers in about 1974, two highly naïve associates—the other was named David Brown—found themselves standing at the back of the crowded room nervously holding guitars. Realizing that singing at a formal Covington lawyers dinner (at which the featured speaker was the quintessentially dignified former Secretary of Defense, Clark Clifford) was not only unprecedented, but possibly foolhardy, David—after it was far too late—whispered, "Homer, this could be a terrible mistake." As the partner-emcee redirected the gaze of the unsuspecting diners to the rear of the room, we launched into two songs, the first parodying the firm's feared and revered senior partner, Tommy Austern, and the other making fun of the firm's recruiting strategy of taking law student recruits to extravagant restaurants with menus most law students couldn't read. Not knowing how to react to such a preposterous stunt, the audience responded not by the death-sentence stony silence we feared, but by standing and applauding.

It probably does not reflect well on one's legal career to name as one of its highlights being applauded by more than 100 distinguished lawyers for singing two silly songs written to tunes by John Prine. But it is what it is, and David Brown and I are still friends. So, too, are the members of that 1975 dinner committee who approved our nonsense in advance: Paul Tagliabue, who later became commissioner of the NFL, and Tom Williamson, who has always wanted just to play in the NFL but instead became president of the D.C. Bar.

The truth is that there were other moments of silly singing (for which the element of surprise is essential, unless you enlist really good singers, like Ricki Tigert, who later became general counsel of the Fed instead). At the Section's first retreat at Amelia Island in 1991, we pilloried in song Ken Reisenfeld's fantasy that the Section hold meetings in Europe (something the Section now does regularly). At Jim Silkenat's instigation at a later retreat, for which I had no responsibility, a very small group of us wound through the audience singing and pantomiming some version of "YMCA." And upon the retirement of Edison Dick, the venerable director of the Section's International Legal Exchange trips for a generation, whose red sport coat we borrowed for the occasion, we sang "I've Got the Trip for You," to a tune stolen from "Guys and Dolls." The lyrics may have been some of my best legal writing.

When doing silly things—not all of which are universally welcomed—it is helpful to keep in mind that not all mistakes and gaffes are career-ending (although, alas, some may be). A public slip of the tongue, an unflattering press item, an argument that a judge excoriates, an ill-timed joke, a demoralizing critique by a senior partner, a futile cold call that still makes you cringe, an email *about* a client inadvertently sent *to* a client—most of these embarrassing occasions are not fatal, but are simply collected in that mental bin of things that you recall only when you wake up during the night. We all know of incidents that we treasure, such as a former colleague who got on the shuttle from New York to Washington and discovered en route that the ocean was on the right side of the plane and, therefore, that Boston, not Washington, lay ahead; or another who appeared for an important oral argument, removed his topcoat, and learned that his suit coat was back in Washington; or a third who distracted himself outside the courthouse before argument by whistling at a nearby passerby who turned out to be the judge in his case. Episodes such as these (only a couple of which are autobiographical) are character-building, although that insight comes only with the passage of time.

Finally, I believe it is healthy to keep in mind that practicing law is not the be-all-and-end-all in life, even when it claims to be. Resisting the voracious appetite that the law business has for one's personal time is not easy. However, life's greatest satisfactions are found in neither the marginal billable hour nor the marginal dollar of compensation. Most are found in diversions and other interests, be they family, music, high mountain ranges, or lowbrow novels (Carl Hiaasen, for example). Smelling flowers and planting trees are worthy endeavors. Learning to use the technology that now stalks us around the clock to gain more time and flexibility has also become a valuable professional skill. And, of course, we all have happy colleagues who, to paraphrase John Kennedy's slanderous comment about the advantages of a Harvard education and a Yale degree, have combined the rewards of a legal education and a nonlegal career. (In recently calling law school classmates for reunion gifts, in quick succession I came upon a priest, a college president, a Wyoming politician, a New York artist, and one adventuresome friend whose career path remains undocumented.)

My advice to any readers who may still be with us is to read the foregoing not for advice or guidance, but as one example of a non-linear legal career that has proved rewarding and enjoyable, much as you might read an obituary of someone you don't know but whose life experiences may cause you to reflect on how you might wish to map your own. Then, if you have a few remaining moments of free time, you could read a poem. Poems by Billy Collins are terrific, and often make you laugh.

Index